DOES THE BIBLE REALLY SAY THAT?
SERIES

GOSPEL OF WEALTH OR POVERTY?

DOES THE BIBLE REALLY SAY THAT? SERIES

GOSPEL OF WEALTH OR POVERTY?

How Do Bible Verses About Jesus, Wealth, Poverty And Heaven Affect Your Income?

Kalinda Rose Stevenson, Ph.D.

ABKA
ABKA Publishing

Limits of Liability/Disclaimer of Warranty

Notice of References to Trademarked Material

The one who tells the stories rules the world.

Hopi Proverb

CONTENTS

PART FIVE WHAT THE MONEY STORIES MEAN FOR YOU

Preface to the Revised Edition

Gospel of Wealth or Poverty? is a book with a publication history. The first version was originally published as an ebook titled *Going Broke with Jesus.* A slightly revised version was then published in both paperback and Kindle versions as *Can a Rich Man Get into Heaven?* In both cases, the title of the book didn't quite catch the intended focus of the book. Both titles made money too much a matter of individual experience even though the purpose of the book has always been to locate personal financial status within the social, political, economic, and religious contexts of the ancient world and of our own.

The Question Mark

Gospel of Wealth or Poverty? draws attention to the connection between your financial status and your biblical beliefs by considering the overlapping and intersecting social, political, economic, and religious contexts of your life. The question mark in the title is the most important element of the title itself—and the most easily overlooked—because it calls into question the either/or choice between wealth or poverty.

Emphasis on Personal Salvation

The emphasis on the overlapping and intersecting social, economic, and religious contexts is contrary to the predominant focus on personal salvation in the contemporary Christian church. Especially in the United States, churches in the last half of the twentieth century and continuing into the twenty-first century have become more about the individual and less about the location of an individual in society. With the rise of evangelicalism and the decline of the older "mainstream" churches, the primary focus shifted from the person within a larger social context to personal salvation of individuals. In evangelicalism, the dominant question is: "Do you accept Jesus as your personal savior?" With this emphasis on personal salvation, religion tends to become a matter of the individual rather than the society.

Although churches still become involved in social justice matters and helping the needy, this focus on the personal salvation of individuals followed the pathway set by the rise of psychotherapy started by Sigmund Freud in the late nineteenth and early twentieth centuries. The result is a shift in primary focus from being part of a society to focus on your self and your relationship with Jesus.

This emphasis on personal salvation doctrine also obscures the social, political, and economic issues that are the foundation of the New Testament Gospel stories. In the New Testament, the stories are not about personal salvation but about the salvation of oppressed people from the injustices of the ruling class.

Why This Matters Now

This focus on contexts is particularly important now. In recent years, the rich have gotten richer. The poor have become poorer. The middle class is slowly disappearing. People who have worked all of their lives have become unemployable. People who thought they were financially secure saw their retirement savings evaporate almost overnight. Homeowners lost their homes while banks increased their profits. Meanwhile, religious beliefs about who deserves and who doesn't deserve wealth have become potent forces to shape political and economic policy. Religious beliefs about money allow the extremely rich to justify both their wealth and the impoverishment of others.

Through it all, wealth has moved upwards, massively increasing the wealth of multibillionaires. At the same time some politicians insist that increasing the minimum wage of the working poor would cost far too much money. The poor are called lazy, unwilling to work, undeserving mooches at the public trough.

Consolidation of wealth in the hands of a tiny few is nothing new in human history. Neither is religious justification for why the rich deserve to be rich and why the poor deserve to be poor. You can find many examples in the Bible that declare that wealth is a sign of God's blessing.

At the same, significant portions of the Bible are profoundly concerned with the economic injustices inflicted by rich rulers against the poor. This is particularly evident in the New Testament Gospel stories of Jesus. In the gospel stories, economic issues are at the heart of the matter.

Gospel of Wealth by Andrew Carnegie

The title *Gospel of Wealth or Poverty?* is partly derived from an essay written by Andrew Carnegie in 1889 in which he addressed the problem of "Rich and Poor." He identifies the problem this way:

> The problem of our age is the proper administration of wealth, so that the ties of brotherhood may still bind together the rich and the poor in harmonious relationship (Carnegie).

The core of his argument is that inherited wealth does no one any good. Rather than leave surplus wealth to families or bequeath it for public purposes, Carnegie's solution was for the rich to administer their wealth during their lifetimes for the benefit of the poor. As "trustees for the poor," the very rich are obligated to use their "superior wisdom" to administer their wealth for the benefit of their "poorer brethren." The title of his essay was "Wealth." The essay became known as the "Gospel of Wealth" based on the last line of the essay.

My purpose is not to analyze Carnegie's solution but to focus on what he saw as the problem for a society when inherited wealth allows the rich to get richer as the poor get poorer.

Income Inequality Now

The problem of income inequality is becoming more obvious each day. On the day that I write this, the best-selling book on Amazon is *Capital in the Twenty-First Century* by French economist Thomas Piketty. The book makes the case that unrestrained capitalism is creating greater income inequality as it erases the more egalitarian distribution of wealth in the twentieth century with the kind of income inequality of the eighteenth and nineteenth centuries.

On the same day, the New York Times article by David Leonhardt and Kevin Quealy makes the case that "The American Middle Class Is No Longer the World's Richest":

> The American middle class, long the most affluent in the world, has lost that distinction.

> While the wealthiest Americans are outpacing many of their global peers, a New York Times analysis shows that across the lower- and middle-income tiers, citizens of other advanced countries have received considerably larger raises over the last three decades (Leonhardt and Quealy).

On the same day, Robert Reich proposes "Raising Taxes on Corporations that Pay Their CEOs Royally and Treat Their Workers Like Serfs":

> Until the 1980s, corporate CEOs were paid, on average, 30 times what their typical worker was paid.

Since then, CEO pay has skyrocketed to 280 times the pay of a typical worker; in big companies, to 354 times (Reich).

On the same day, Bill Moyers claims that "Government = Protection Racket for the 1 Percent":

The evidence of income inequality just keeps mounting. According to "Working for the Few," a recent briefing paper from Oxfam, "In the US, the wealthiest one percent captured 95 percent of post-financial crisis growth since 2009, while the bottom 90 percent became poorer."

...

And at state and local levels, while the poorest *fifth* of Americans pay an average tax rate of over 11 percent, the richest one percent of the country pay -- are you ready for this? -- half that rate (Moyers).

A Socioeconomic Perspective on the Bible

These articles are just the tip of the iceberg about the growing inequity between the rich and the poor and income stagnation of the middle. In such a time as ours, it's time for a fresh socioeconomic perspective on what the Bible really says about wealth and poverty. The dominant tendencies to focus on Bible verses and personal salvation have obscured how much the gap between the rich and poor is at the heart of the New Testament gospel stories.

Gospel of Wealth or Poverty? puts Bible verses about Jesus and money in the social, political, economic, and religious contexts of ancient Palestine. In these ancient contexts, the rich get richer, the poor get poorer, wealth flows upwards, and the poor pay taxes at a higher tax rate than the rich.

In other words, what Jesus says about money in the Gospel stories of the New Testament demonstrates striking similarities as well as dramatic differences between the world of Jesus and the world of the early twenty-first century.

Above all, this means that wealth and poverty are not just personal matters. Whatever your own relationship with money, whether you are struggling, whether you are rich, or whether you are somewhere in the middle, money is never simply a personal matter. Money is always a social matter.

A Gospel of Poverty?

One more preliminary detail concerns poverty. The phrase "Gospel of Wealth" comes from Carnegie. However, consideration of wealth is not enough without considering poverty. The contrast between rich and poor and the role of the few to use their wealth to create poverty for the many is a significant theme in the Gospel stories.

What is most significant is that Jesus does not hold out the promise of wealth to his followers. Despite the claims of prosperity gospel preachers, in the New Testament gospel stories, Jesus is not a rich man preaching a gospel of wealth. He does not say, "Follow me and get rich." Rather, he calls his disciples to a life of poverty. This is a call that few are willing to accept in the biblical stories and in our contemporary world.

Gospel of Wealth or Poverty? is about what Jesus *really said* about money and what Jesus *really didn't say* about money in the New Testament Gospel stories. It puts money in social, political, economic, and religious contexts, which is where we all live our lives. You cannot grasp the full significance of anything Jesus said in the New Testament gospels by isolating Bible verses about money from the larger contexts of story and society.

If you are a Christian believer who reads the Bible to find out "what Jesus says about money" as a guide for your own relationship with money, you are faced with this dichotomy between "a gospel of wealth" and "a gospel of poverty." How do you come to terms with what Jesus said about the rich and poor and about wealth and poverty? How do you reconcile the claims of prosperity gospel preachers with much Christian teaching about the evils of money? How do you reconcile "what the Bible says about money" with the economic realities of life in the twenty-first century?

If you are not a Christian believer but you have been exposed to enough statements about "what Jesus says about money," you might experience the same nagging questions. Christian beliefs about money are pervasive, subliminal, and rarely questioned.

The primary question in all of this is: Is there another choice beyond the either/or of wealth or poverty that is so characteristic of various Christian claims about the Bible and money?

Gospel of Wealth or Poverty? calls into the question the dichotomy itself and offers another perspective to move beyond this either/or choice of wealth or poverty. This new perspective is profoundly biblical but doesn't require you to "believe" anything about the Bible. It is a perspective that sets your relationship with money within the larger social, political, economic, and religious contexts of your life in the twenty-first century.

Preface

Does the Bible Really Say That? Series

Gospel of Wealth or Poverty? is part of the Does The Bible Really Say That? Series. The purpose of the series is to identify some of the most frequently misunderstood Bible verses to demonstrate why the Bible often doesn't say what you think it says.

The focus is not on the truth of the Bible itself but the impact of claims about "what the Bible says" on Bible readers.

Bible believers study the Bible as the authoritative guide to their lives. Non-believers quote the Bible to ridicule its claims or denounce its relevance to contemporary life. Both believers and non-believers alike use the language of "the Bible says" to make their claims.

The books in this series are not typical Bible studies. They do not promote or deny faith in God, Jesus, or any part of the Bible and they make no claims about whether or not any part of the Bible is historically true or false. Instead, they intend to refute *unbiblical* claims about the Bible that are often accepted without challenge as *biblical* by believers and non-believers alike.

Three Problems with "The Bible Says"

Does the Bible Really Say That? books focus on three foundational problems with the language of "the Bible says."

The first problem concerns *translation*. Unless readers are able to read the Bible in its original languages, all claims about "what the Bible says" are based on translations of ancient documents. The result is that original meanings get lost in translation. What "the Bible says" in its original languages is not always what translations claim that "the Bible says" on any particular topic.

The second problem concerns *Bible verses*. The Bible was not written as a collection of Bible verses. It is made up of whole stories within whole books. When whole stories are chopped up into separate verses, and the verses are then treated as stand-alone units, the result is a contradictory set of beliefs about what is "biblical" and what is not.

The third problem concerns *context*. No part of the Bible was written apart from its own literary, social, political, historical, religious, and linguistic contexts. When Bible verses are treated as isolated units, they lose all connection with their original contexts and become proof texts to be applied in other contexts.

The intention of the series is provide a way to undo the harm done to innocent and vulnerable people by mistranslated, misquoted, and misunderstood Bible verses that result in self-conflict, confusion, abuse, shame, and abiding conflict about money.

Hero's Journeys

An essential feature of *Gospel of Wealth or Poverty?* is the concept of the *hero's journey*. The essential element in a hero's journey is that the journey is never just about what the hero wants. A hero's journey is always about saving someone or something from a threat.

The primary focus of *Gospel of Wealth or Poverty?* is money. *Gospel of Wealth or Poverty?* describes Jesus' hero's journey concerning economic injustice. When you read the gospel stories this way, they can become models for your own hero's journey concerning your relationship with money.

Money is such a charged topic in our world and especially in the Christian church that even the idea that you could use money heroically might seem like an impossible contradiction between the presumed selflessness of a hero and the presumed selfishness of a rich person.

When the words of Jesus about money are isolated from the whole story of the hero's journey of Jesus, they become Bible verses about the evils or the blessings of money. Then "what Jesus said about money" turns heroism into powerlessness or into privilege, depending on which Bible verses you choose and how you interpret them.

Whether you experience money guilt or money greed, whether you believe in lack of money or abundance of money as God's will for your life, you deserve better than this kind of either/or approach to money based on misunderstood, mistranslated, and misquoted *texts-without-contexts* Bible verses.

Introduction

Either/Or

Wealth and poverty are significant themes in the Bible. They are particularly significant themes in the Gospel stories about Jesus. The worldview of Jesus is of a world with no middle. It is a dichotomous worldview of either/or.

Gospel of Wealth or Poverty? adopts this either/or approach to focus on eight specific statements about wealth and poverty in the New Testament gospels. This focus involves these either/or pairs about use of the Bible:

Bible stories or Bible verses

Heroic Bible stories or Biblical urban legends

Liberating Bible or Constraining Bible

Liberating or Constraining Bible?

The most important either/or contrast is the difference between *Liberating Bible* and *Constraining Bible*. This distinction concerns the use of the Bible and how it impacts you. Does what you read in the Bible liberate you or does it constrain you?

Liberating Bible liberates. The word comes from the Latin *liber*. It means "free, unrestricted, unimpeded." It can also have the negative connotations of "unbridled, unchecked, licentious" (*Online Etymology,* liberal).

Constraining Bible has the opposite effect. The word *constrain* also comes from Latin. It means "with strain." The word combines "com" (together) with the root *stringere,* the source of the English word "string." Strings tie things together. "Strain" means to "tie, bind, fasten" *(Online Etymology,* strain).

To be constrained is to be tied, compressed, fastened, bound, drawn together, pressed, squeezed, constricted, and restricted. English has many words to describe the effect of being constrained, probably because most of us feel constrained far more than we feel free.

Some linguists derive the words "religion" and "obligation" from the Latin *ligare* "to bind" (*Online Etymology,* rely). These meanings also convey the sense of being tied up. Religion has that effect on many people.

Constraining Bible can tie you up in knots, in a state of constant concern about whether you are following the rules. When it comes to money, *Constraining Bible* can keep you stuck between your need and desire to have money and your beliefs that money is evil and you have to choose between God or money.

Constraining Bible has that effect because it focuses on Bible verses rather than whole stories. Most of what people "know" about the Bible comes in the form of Bible verses that are disconnected from the contexts of original Bible stories

Doctrines, rules, beliefs, and practices created from out-of-context Bible verses ignore the linguistic, social, political, historical, geographical, economic, and story contexts of the ancient writings in the Bible. These out-of-context Bible verses then become the foundation of a new type of story—*a biblical urban legend.*

Biblical Urban Legends

Urban legends usually begin with some element of truth and then become untrue as they take on lives of their own. Urban legends are designed to create fear in those who hear them.

When Bible verses follow a similar process, they turn into *biblical urban legends.* They begin with specific meanings in particular contexts and then take on new meanings as they are taken out of original contexts to mean something else. Then these misquoted, misunderstood, and mistranslated Bible verses create fear and limitation in the vulnerable. At the time, they become weapons of power against the poor and vulnerable. Disconnected Bible verses turned into biblical urban legends also allow people with power and privilege to justify their wealth.

The Method

The eight specific statements about money cover a range of social, religious, economic, and political issues. They are all well-known and frequently cited for "what the Bible says" about a range of topics.

We'll look briefly at the *Constraining Bible* biblical urban legends created about them, locate each story in its own original contexts, and then consider a *Liberating Bible* perspective on each of them.

This kind of contextual analysis is a necessary first step before deciding what they mean in the twenty-first century, particularly in the United States of America.

This focus is particularly relevant right now. In the United States and in other countries around the world, the economic crises of 2008 made visible the growing gap between the rich and the poor as well as the impact on the shrinking middle class.

The foundational premise of *Gospel of Wealth or Poverty?* is that Bible stories that were originally intended to be liberating have become constraining biblical urban legends.

Structure of the Book

Part One: Liberating or Constraining Bible Stories considers the impact of Bible stories and verses about money on your life:

- Chapter 1: "Bible Stories That Rule the World" defines two types of stories and how those story types affect your life.

- Chapter 2: "Bible Reading for Adults" considers the life-long impact of learning Bible stories as children and how an adult perspective on Bible stories can change your life.

- Chapter 3: "Stuck in the Eye of the Needle" looks at various interpretations of the encounter between Jesus and a rich man to introduce the concept of a *biblical urban legend*.

Part Two: Society and Stories focuses on the importance of context for understanding Bible verses about money:

- Chapter 4: "Verses versus Verses" demonstrates why opposing opinions about Bible verses result from ignoring the social and story contexts of Bible stories.

- Chapter 5: "Follow the Money" compares and contrasts biblical economic, political, and religious realities with contemporary culture, particularly American culture.

Part Three: Stories of the Outlaw Hero introduces the idea of a hero's journey to describe the gospel stories about Jesus:

- Chapter 6: "Reclaiming The Gospels as Stories" identifies the New Testament Gospels as heroic stories.

- Chapter 7: "Hero's Journeys of the Kingdom" introduces the essential idea of the kingdom of heaven/kingdom of God within the Christian gospel stories.

- Chapter 8: "Jesus the Outlaw Hero" compares the gospel stories about Jesus to outlaw hero's journey stories.

- Chapter 9: "Jesus Confronts the Threat" identifies the threat in the Gospel stories that motivates the hero's journey of Jesus.

Part Four: Money Stories of Jesus looks at eight specific statements about money by Jesus in the gospel stories by putting them in the whole story context of ancient Palestine:

- Chapter 10 "God and Mammon" from the Sermon on the Mount.

- Chapter 11 "Bread and Debts" from the Lord's Prayer.

- Chapter 12: "Blessed Are the Poor" from the Beatitudes.

- Chapter 13: "Taxes to Caesar" about the relationship between religion and government.

- Chapter 14: "The Money Changers" about the economic functions of the temple.

- Chapter 15: "Honor Your Father and Your Mother" about family structure and financial obligations.

- Chapter 16: "The Poor Widow" about the abuse of economic power by religious authorities.

- Chapter 17: "The Rich Young Man" about discipleship in the kingdom of heaven.

Part Five: Money Stories and You considers what Bible stories about money mean for you:

- Chapter 18: "Money Is Power" focuses on how religious teaching about money can rob you of your economic wellbeing.

- Chapter 19: "Your Heroic Money Journey" invites you to choose to become heroic about money.

Conclusion:

- The conclusion makes it personal by asking the "So What?" question about what any of this means for you.

Part One

Constraining

or

Liberating

Bible Stories

Chapter 1
Bible Stories That Rule the World

The one who tells the stories rules the
world.

Hopi Proverb

The epigraph at the beginning of the book is not only a
signpost pointing out the theme of the book. It also defines
the crux of the problem. It identifies the power of stories to
rule the world. Stories rule the world because they teach us
who we are and how we are to live. Most significantly, it
identifies the one who tells the stories as the one with
power to rule our lives.

One of my writing teachers, Hal Zina Bennett, taught a
basic principle about writing. He claimed that the more
particular and personal the story, the more universal the
story becomes:

To tell the story of the moments when we've
suffered and then healed our essential wounds is to
reveal a universal insight that extends far beyond the
particulars (Bennet 109).

And so before I do anything else, I will tell a particular and
personal story. After I relate the story, I will tell you more
about my intention for this book, and how stories can heal
even the deepest suffering.

It's no accident that my story begins with a story that
was intended to teach me how to live in the world. This
particular story was the topic of a Sunday School lesson
when I was in the second grade. Every week, we had a
different story in our lesson books. Each story had color
illustrations about the characters in the story. After we

9

read the story, the teacher talked with us about what we were supposed to learn from the story.

In the story, a blue-eyed blond girl, who was just my age, visited an Indian reservation in the Southwest with her parents. The girl had just received a brand new doll for her birthday. She loved the beautiful doll. At the reservation, she saw a little Indian girl. The Indian girl also had a doll, but her doll was crude, made of corncobs, straw, and coarse cloth. The blue-eyed girl felt sorry for the poor Indian girl with her homemade doll and so she gave her beautiful, brand new doll to the Indian girl. In gratitude for such generosity, the Indian girl gave her crude, homemade doll to the blue-eyed girl. The illustration showed the blue-eyed girl's parents beaming with pride as the two girls exchanged their dolls.

The story ended with the moral of the story. This is what God wanted from us. This is what Jesus taught us to do. We were supposed to serve the poor by giving away the best that we had. Since I was also a blue-eyed, blond girl, I identified strongly with the good little girl in the story.

I don't remember the teacher's comments about the story, but I am sure they were no different from what I was told Sunday after Sunday for much of my childhood. God wanted us to be good. Being good meant helping others, giving to the poor, and being obedient to authority.

Soon after this Sunday School lesson, I visited my friend Linda after school. In my elementary school, visiting a friend on a different bus route was a complicated process, involving both written and unwritten rules. It involved a permission slip to ride a different school bus. For girls, it also involved an unwritten rule that the visiting girl was supposed to take her doll to school.

As a naturally athletic girl—a tomboy—who loved to climb trees, play baseball, swim, ice skate, ride my bike, and do cartwheels on the lawn, I was never very interested in playing with dolls. However, my lack of interest in dolls didn't change the fact that I was a girl and a girl *had* to have a doll and I *had* to take my doll to school to visit Linda.

Not long before my visit to Linda, my mother made a snowsuit for my doll. My mother was a talented seamstress who produced exceptional creations. The snowsuit was blue—my favorite color—one piece, fully lined, with a set-in zipper and black cuffs for both the sleeves and the pant legs, and a collar of the same material as the cuffs. It even had an embroidered design in black thread on the front. The doll's snowsuit was a work of art.

The same winter my mother made the snowsuit for my doll, I went to school every day wearing an ugly hand-me-down gray jacket with two missing buttons and a torn cuff on one sleeve. Since girls had to wear dresses to school, we also wore snowpants on the coldest days. My snowpants were hand-me-downs from an older brother. They were dark brown and were missing one cuff, which meant that one leg took on a fair bit of snow that winter.

I remember looking at the doll's beautiful snowsuit and thinking that the doll was much better dressed than I was.

But none of that mattered on the appointed day of the visit. I took my well-dressed doll to school in her beautiful blue snowsuit and rode the bus to Linda's house, where Linda followed protocol and brought out her doll. I immediately noticed that her doll was wearing an old cotton dress.

With the Sunday School story still in my mind, I decided to give the snowsuit to Linda. In return, Linda gave me the cotton dress. I knew that I was giving away the best I had for the equivalent of a doll made of corncobs and straw that was dressed in rags. I was doing what I was supposed to do. I was being good.

The flaw in my plan was that my mother had not read the Sunday School story. She didn't know that she was supposed to congratulate me for being so good. Unlike the parents in the story, who beamed with pride at their daughter's selflessness, my mother was furious when I showed her the cotton dress I received in exchange for the snowsuit.

From my mother's perspective, giving away the snowsuit was more proof of my selfishness and ingratitude. It demonstrated one once again that I never appreciated anything she did for me. I never heard the end of the snowsuit episode until I escaped from that house on the day after my eighteenth birthday.

Two Types of Stories

Stories do rule the world. Broadly speaking, there are two types of stories—stories that *constrain* you and stories that *liberate* you.

Constraining stories teach you to shrink and shrivel, to worry about breaking rules, to learn your place, and keep you obedient. They are morality tales about the dangers of stepping out of line.

In contrast, *liberating stories* teach you to grow, to risk, to dare, to go beyond your current limits. They are *heroic stories* that plant visions of possibilities that appeal to the best within us.

The hero looks at the world and says: "Something is wrong here. Someone needs to do something about it. And I am that someone." A hero is the one who faces fear and obstacles to make things right. This is what heroes do. They always act for something bigger than themselves, to make life better for others as well as themselves.

The essential wound for many of us who grew up with some sort of Christian religious education is that we were taught Bible stories as morality tales rather than heroic stories. Instead of teaching us to be brave, we were taught to be afraid. Instead of teaching us to confront oppressive abuse of power, we were taught to be obedient to power.

Instead of teaching us to trust ourselves, we were taught to be helpless.

The Jesus portrayed in the New Testament gospel stories was a hero. He did what heroes do. He stood in the face of oppressive authority to advocate for a more just world.

Yet, the Jesus I learned about as a scared child in Sunday school was not very heroic. He was "meek and mild," submissive, obedient, doing God's will. We were told that Jesus was the perfect example of obedience.

Constraining Bible and Liberating Bible

This leads me to the fundamental point of the book. *Gospel of Wealth or Poverty?* is about the difference between *Liberating Bible* stories and *Constraining Bible* stories concerning money.

The designation *Constraining Bible* is not a judgment about the Bible itself. Instead, *Constraining Bible* refers to the use of the Bible as a weapon of power that constrains others. One primary weapon of power refers to economic power of the rich to increase the wealth of the rich by increasing the poverty of the poor.

In contrast, the designation *Liberating Bible* concerns freedom from abusive power. Liberation is not license. Liberation doesn't give you freedom to act however you want to act or do whatever you want to do if your actions constrain others:

- *Constraining Bible* turns heroic stories into moralistic lessons to teach that poverty is God's will for the poor.

- *Liberating Bible* focuses on heroic actions against the rich who impoverish the poor.

- *Constraining Bible* stories teach fear, lack, and limitation in the name of God.

- *Liberating Bible* stories teach courage, abundance, and trust in the name of God.

- *Constraining Bible* stories demand obedience to those who misuse their power as God's will.

- *Liberating Bible* stories demand justice by challenging abusive authority as contrary to God's highest intention.

- *Constraining Bible* stories create doubt and self-hatred, all the while claiming the love of God.

- *Liberating Bible* stories create trust and compassion for self and others as evidence of the love of God.

The Effect of Constraining Bible

Constraining Bible operates within a constricted vision of human life. It sees life on earth as a test of obedience to God's rules based on the claim that these rules are clearly defined in the Bible.

With this focus, human life becomes an obedience test for sinners. The ultimate goal of human life is heavenly salvation. Therefore, "getting into heaven" is the carrot at the end of the stick. If you obey the rules, if you do what you are commanded to do and don't do what you are commanded not to do, and if you ask forgiveness for your sins and your sinful nature, you will *probably* be admitted to heaven.

With this *Constraining Bible* vision of human life, the Bible becomes the ultimate rulebook for life on earth. What you must do and what you must not do is clearly defined in its pages. The Bible is therefore the only *infallible* guide to life and practice.

With this vision of "life as an obedience test" and the Bible as the ultimate source of God's rules, *Constraining*

Bible stories focus heavily on matters of *authority*. Authority is defined by roles, sex, age, and social status. Who has authority? Who must obey authority? The *Constraining Bible* storytellers will tell you.

Constraining Bible is defined by limitations, restrictions, and exclusions as it separates the ones who will be "saved" from the ones who will not. Salvation depends upon obedience to the rules laid out in the Bible.

What is the effect of this *Constraining Bible* emphasis on following rules and obedience to authority? *Constraining Bible* produces fear, doubt, anxiety, guilt, and shame in the vulnerable. They are the ones who are told that they are not worthy of salvation but can be saved if they are sufficiently obedient to the authority of the Bible and the ones who have God's authority to rule over them.

How did the Bible become *Constraining Bible*? This kind of use of the Bible tends to be a distinctly Protestant phenomenon. As part of the Protestant Reformation, ultimate authority for determining God's will for human life was displaced from the Roman Catholic hierarchy to the Bible itself.

The claim that the Bible is without error and the only infallible guide in faith and practice is a relatively new phenomenon in Christian history. It began in the late nineteenth century in the United States and became the foundation of fundamentalism and evangelicalism in the twentieth century. For such believers, this claim that the Bible is error-free and the only infallible guide to faith and practice invests the Bible with singular authority over Christian life.

Visions of Liberation

In contrast, *Liberating Bible* sees life on earth as a gift to be lived rather than an obedience test. It offers visions of wholeness, blessing, and love that liberate the unfree from fear, lack, doubt, guilt, and shame. It concerns justice and wellbeing for yourself and others here and now. It teaches heroism rather than obedience. It teaches a willingness to stand against the misuse of power that makes life miserable for others.

My purpose is to demonstrate how much of this *Constraining Bible* focus is unbiblical. This can be your first step in liberating yourself from the influence of *Constraining Bible* morality tales about money. When you realize how many claims about "what the Bible says" are actually unbiblical, you can free yourself from oppressive misuse of the Bible.

Let me be as clear as possible. This is not a book about faith. I am neither promoting nor challenging faith in Jesus as the Son of God. Instead, it is a book about the stories of Jesus concerning money and the impact of those stories upon those of us who learned morality tales instead of hero's stories in our Christian education. I intend this book to demolish the morality tales and reclaim the hero's stories behind the words of Jesus about money. I have no interest in demolishing anyone's faith in Jesus as the Christ.

Joe versus the Volcano is one of my favorite movies. It's a movie that is both silly and profound as it traces Joe's hero's journey. Joe, played by Tom Hanks, is called to his heroic journey by the ultra-rich Mr. Graynamore, played by Lloyd Bridges. Mr. Graynamore peers into Joe's eyes and says:

I'm trying to see the hero in there.

This book is about retelling the stories of Jesus about money so that you can see the hero within yourself and set out on your own heroic money journey.

Chapter 2
Bible Reading For Adults

The greatest obstacle to liberating people from Bible stories told as morality tales is that most of us first learned Bible stories as children. M. Scott Peck's statement is a powerful commentary on the religious education of children:

> I sometimes tell people that one of the great blessings of my life was an almost total absence of religious education, because I had nothing to overcome (Peck 113).

Unlike Peck, many of us who learned about money in Sunday school and church have a whole lot to overcome.

Why do early beliefs, which we learned as children, have such lasting power in our lives? Memorizing Bible verses is a large part of the problem. A very young child is pure emotion, incapable of understanding abstract concepts. As young children, we had no capacity to differentiate and evaluate the lessons we learned. We took words literally and applied them directly to our own young lives. We had no larger context to explain or understand the experiences of our lives.

In addition, our teachers taught us with songs and stories and pictures, all methods guaranteed to embed the lessons deeply into our conscious and subconscious minds. When we memorized Bible verses, without any critical capacity to understand the true meaning of the words, the words themselves became part of our subconscious emotional nature, taking root for a lifetime unless we consciously weed them out.

One of the Bible verses many children learn in Sunday School is "the love chapter" from First Corinthians 13:

> When I was a child, I spoke like a child, I thought like a child, I reasoned like a child; when I became a man, I gave up childish ways (1 Corinthians 13:11, Revised Standard Version).

The statement by the Apostle Paul indicates that a necessary part of becoming an adult is to give up childish thinking.

And so, the first step in putting the heroic back into the Bible stories is to read the Bible as adults. Yet, those who rule the world by controlling the stories often have a vested interest in treating adults as children.

I first encountered this attitude as a student in theological seminary. Seminaries are professional schools that train clergy of all denominations. Seminary students are college graduates, many coming to seminary after other careers.

Discovering the Secrets

During my first semester as a seminary student, I took my first course in Biblical Greek. As I learned Greek, I began to think that I had somehow managed to join a secret society. As one of a handful of women among more than seven hundred male students, I experienced great hostility from some students who were convinced that women had no place in seminary. They justified their hostility by quoting Bible verses claiming that women have no authority to teach—verses I now know have been wrongly translated.

But even with all of that painful drama, I began to realize that the scholars who could read Greek knew secrets that they were not willing to share with the people sitting in churches on Sunday mornings. The next year, when I began to learn Hebrew, I grew more aware that the people who could read Greek and Hebrew knew more than they were telling.

Even as a beginning student, I saw misleading translations. I saw words added in translations and taken out of translations to perpetuate traditional readings. The ones who could read Greek and Hebrew knew better. But they were keeping the secrets.

It wasn't just reading Greek and Hebrew that made the difference. I learned about manuscript traditions. I learned about the differences between ancient writings and modern books. I learned about the problems of translating ancient languages into modern languages. I saw how we have imposed English language meanings into Biblical readings. In all of this, I saw more and more how the professional scholars knew secrets they weren't telling the people in churches.

Our teachers would sometimes comment: "Don't tell the people in the churches about this. You'll destroy their faith."

I decided very early that I would have no part of that game. I thought that adults deserve to be treated as adults. During my internship year, when I first preached and taught in church, I taught what I knew, as well as I knew how to teach it.

Encountering Resistance

Yet the resistance to teaching the truth about the Bible runs in both directions. One of the reasons that scholars resist telling the people what they know is that scholars have too often been treated as heretics when they challenge childish notions about the Bible.

As a doctoral student in Biblical studies, I was a teaching assistant before I began to teach my own classes. Many times, I attempted to bring an adult perspective to adult students who were acting like two-year olds having temper tantrums or to crying students who lamented that their faith had been "destroyed" because of something a professor said in class. The professors were simply translating what was clear in the Greek or the Hebrew. As a result, they became targets for student outrage. Some of the students took this as proof that what they had been warned about was really true: "Seminaries are cemeteries of faith."

This brings me to my greatest challenge in this book. How can I use my biblical studies scholarship in a way that reveals the heroic stories behind Sunday School morality tales?

One of my early readers told me: "Leave out the scholarship. People don't want to know all of that stuff." Other early readers were amazed at what the scholarship revealed to them about the meanings behind familiar Bible verses.

From my perspective, scholarship is what set me free from the well-meaning Sunday school lessons that taught me to be "good" instead of heroic. If I leave out the scholarship, I will leave out the best I have to offer.

I believe profoundly that the scholarship will liberate you from the kind of Sunday School teaching that told me that God wanted me to give away the doll's snowsuit for an old cotton doll's dress.

So, I have attempted to include scholarship in a way that is clear and genuinely helpful. My goal is to set you free from the kind of *Constraining Bible* reading that treats you as a disobedient little child who needs to be told what is good for you.

I trust you. If you can read this book, you are an adult who deserves to be treated as an adult, especially concerning money and the Bible. I promise you that nothing in this book will destroy your faith in God or Jesus as the Son of God. I also promise you that much in this book will set you free from the morality tales that obscure the liberating intent of the Christian gospel stories. My goal is to set you free from *Constraining Bible* so that you can discover what the Bible actually says about money.

The basic problem is that most of us learned about money from out-of-context Bible verses. The only liberating solution is to put the Bible verses into context to determine what they meant in the gospel narratives.

About Translation

Although I love to do my own translations, I have used the *Revised Standard Version* throughout. The *Revised Standard Version* was first published in 1952. It was a revision of the *American Standard Version*, published in 1901, which was a revision of the *King James Version*, published in 1611. Although there are more recent translations, including the *New Revised Standard Version*, published in 1989, I have chosen the Revised Standard to use familiar language without reproducing the archaic English of the *King James Version*. For the most familiar passages, I have also included the *King James Version*.

The *Revised Standard Version* was an attempt to retain the familiar cadences and language of the *King James Version* at the same time that it replaced some of the outdated English with contemporary American language. The *Revised Standard Version* also used biblical manuscripts the King James translators did not have.

In the sixty-plus years since the *Revised Standard Version* was published, there have been other translations. Most have much to recommend them. All have weaknesses. Every translation is subject to the same limitations as any effort to translate from one language to another.

A significant hazard for people who commit themselves to be obedient to Biblical authority is that they rarely understand how often the translations have misled them. I have seen instances of people who attempt to align their lives with Bible verses without realizing that they are committing themselves to something that was badly translated. No matter how diligently translators commit themselves to translating accurately, translators sometimes mistranslate.

Translation involves hard, hard work. It requires substantial effort to understand what original writings meant in their own contexts. It also requires substantial effort to put original meanings into contemporary language in a way that accurately represents the intention of the originals.

After all of the hard work, no translation can last forever. Scholars continue to understand more about what the original words meant in their own contexts. Meanwhile, no language stands still, especially a language such as English, which is constantly growing and evolving.

As a way of putting it all into perspective, I offer a vivid image from my first year of theological seminary. One of my New Testament professors—a man given to flamboyant gestures—stood in front of the lecture hall, waving the Greek New Testament in his hand and declared: "This is the New Testament. Every thing else is a translation." This is an essential insight into anything you read in the Bible. Unless you are reading the Bible in its original Greek and Hebrew—and the few words here and there in Aramaic— you are reading a translation. Translations are always subject to question and revision.

Chapter 3
Stuck in the Eye of the Needle

And Jesus said to his disciples, "Truly, I say to you, it will be hard for a rich man to enter the kingdom of heaven. Again I tell you, it is easier for a camel to go through the eye of a needle than for a rich man to enter the kingdom of God" (Matthew 19: 23-24, Revised Standard Version).

I once attended a seminar about creating a millionaire mindset about money. After a break, I was returning to my seat when I saw one of the students talking with the speaker. The speaker was standing on the platform looking down. The student was standing on the floor looking up. Before I heard what they were talking about, I thought about how hard it would be to have a heart-to-heart, eye-to-eye conversation with such a difference in elevation between them.

As I got closer, I heard the student ask: "How can you say it's good to be rich? Jesus said that a rich man can't get into heaven." The speaker looked down at the man and said: "That's just an allegorical story about being greedy. If you're not greedy, there is nothing wrong with being rich."

Anyone who teaches or speaks knows that sometimes people ask questions that are not real questions. They want to trap you or simply express an opinion. And sometimes people ask questions that lay their hearts bare. The man looking up at the speaker was asking that kind of question. He was clearly distressed and seeking an answer.

Making Up Stories about the Bible

This fragment of a conversation demonstrates what happens when two people of widely divergent religious backgrounds converge on one Bible verse. They might be talking about the same Bible verse but they are universes apart in understanding.

Yet, this brief conversation gets to the heart of my reason for this book—the difference between heroic stories and morality tales.

The most basic difference between the two types of stories is the purpose behind them:

- Heroic stories concern solving problems. Morality tales concern right behavior.

- Heroic tales often require the hero to break the rules to solve the problem. Morality tales exist to teach obedience to the rules.

This difference is why:

- Heroic stories empower while morality tales disempower.

- Heroic stories lead to boldness in the service of some greater purpose while morality tales lead to meekness in service of self-preservation.

- Heroic stories create courage to overcome limitations while morality tales create fear of violating authority.

Missing the Point

In this one brief conversation, both the speaker and the questioner expressed beliefs based on a few words cut adrift from the context of the original story. Each of these two men had made up a story about Jesus and money. Neither one had made up a heroic story about money. Each one treated the words of Jesus as a morality tale about money. Each in his own way had missed the fundamental point of the story behind the words.

The distressed questioner had misquoted the verse itself. Jesus did not say that "a rich man can't get into heaven." In the three biblical versions of the story, Jesus made a statement about a rich man entering the *kingdom of God* or *kingdom of heaven*. By identifying the kingdom of heaven with heaven, the questioner had significantly missed the point of the story.

For his part, the speaker claimed that Jesus was using an allegory to teach a lesson about greed. *Allegory* is just another way to describe a morality tale. He assured the questioner that there was nothing wrong with being rich as long as he wasn't greedy. The language of "there's nothing wrong with" is a clear sign of a moralistic reading of a story. By treating the story as an allegory—a morality tale—about personal morality, the speaker had also missed the fundamental point of the story.

So, within the brief conversation, we have one man in conflict over a misquoted Bible verse and a teacher who dismissed the question with an answer that turned a biblical story about an unjust society into a moralistic statement about greed.

When the words of Jesus to the rich man are put into the context of the story itself, it's clear that what Jesus had to say about the rich man was part of his condemnation of an oppressive economic system.

What the Bible "Means" Depends on Where You Stand

This brief episode between two men who were standing just inches from each other, but were miles apart in understanding, encapsulates the challenge of any kind of claim about "what Jesus said about money." It's so easy to turn any discussion about the Bible into confident assertions about "what the Bible really says" without stopping to consider that what you think the words mean depends on where you stand and what you bring to the question.

Money or Heaven

I didn't know the man who asked the question but I instantly felt compassion for him. I knew what he was asking. He was asking to be set free from his conflict between his desire for salvation and his desire for money.

He asked about the words of Jesus that a "rich man can't get into heaven." The answer he got—that the story is an allegory about greed—didn't address his unexpressed question. The unexpressed question was: "Will I get into heaven if I am rich?

The man clearly believed that Jesus taught that a rich man can't get into heaven. How could he reconcile what he thought Jesus was saying in the Bible with a desire to develop a millionaire mindset?

The speaker's answer couldn't and didn't address the real issue. When the speaker dismissed the question with the assertion, "It is just an allegory about greed," he gave no indication that he understood how important the question was to the questioner.

In that setting, no one could have answered this question. Certainly not a speaker who was besieged by questions during a fifteen-minute break. The only one who could possibly grasp the importance of this question is someone who has lived with fear of getting it wrong.

Religion and Authority

The root meaning of the word *religion* is to *tie back*. People who are not bound by belief in the authority of the Bible over their lives cannot grasp how much power Bible verses have in the lives of some believers.

People who have spent any part of their lives immersed in a culture shaped by biblical authority know all too well the power of Bible verses. They also understand how fearful it is to challenge the authority of the Bible over their lives.

Whether such people received their Bible training in Sunday School, church, or a Bible-based cult, any perceived challenge to biblical authority is dangerous. If you believe that your salvation depends on obedience to the words of the Bible, it's no help at all to hear that that Jesus was making an allegory about greed rather than a claim about heaven. From this perspective, to challenge the words of Jesus in the Bible is to risk salvation itself.

Bible Verses and Obligation

People have a lot of reasons for studying the Bible. My reason was to set myself free from the ties created by Bible verses. My own bondage was to verses about obedience to my abusive parents. I was terrified by the people in my life. I was even more terrified that God would punish me if I didn't do what the Bible verses told me I had to do.

I first learned about the Bible the way most people learn about the Bible. I learned Bible verses. Snippets. Fragments. Sayings. They filled me with obligations. The word *obligation* comes from the same root as *religion*. Religion *ties back*. Obligation *ties to*.

My Reasons for Writing This Book

One of the reasons I am writing this book is to answer compelling questions, such as the one the man asked the speaker. He asked the most important question he could ask and he got an answer that didn't even address the real question behind his words: "Will I get into heaven if I am rich?"

This book is my effort to answer such questions by demonstrating how much the man had completely misunderstood the verse and misused the words.

As a biblical scholar, who has spent much of my adult life immersed in biblical study, I know that there are more liberating answers to such questions than the one the man heard at the seminar. I do not take the task lightly.

Bible Verses

Any solution that answers the kinds of questions the man at the seminar asked cannot start by quoting Bible verses. It is a demonstration of pious hocus-pocus that many Christians who believe that the Bible is "Good News" use Bible verses in a way to keep people *tied back* to beliefs that do more harm than good.

Bible verses by themselves rarely set people free. Instead, they often create bondage to biblical interpretations that keep people stuck, afraid, struggling, and broke.

Biblical Urban Legends

Up to this point, I have contrasted heroic stories and morality tales. Now, let's look at a particular type of morality tale. A *morality tale* concerns right behavior. A morality tale with a warning is a *cautionary tale*. Throughout human history, human beings have used cautionary tales to warn, persuade, and frighten people against danger. Cautionary tales describe the fearful consequences of stepping out of line.

My name for a cautionary tale based on Bible verses is a *biblical urban legend*. You might be wondering: What does the term, *biblical urban legend* add to the discussion beyond the idea of a cautionary tale?

Most of us understand the idea of urban legends. An *urban legend* usually starts out with some element of truth.

It becomes false as it is told and retold. Urban legends thrive in our contemporary world, especially in the era of the internet, where they proliferate. Usually, a tell-tale sign of an online urban legend is the urgent warning about some event that is about to occur. The warning comes with instructions to forward the message to everyone you know.

In other words, urban legends are cautionary tales set in our contemporary era. The only difference between urban legends and cautionary tales told as fables, parables, and tall tales is that urban legends are cautionary tales set in the contemporary world. Instead of cautionary tales about mythic creatures such as dragons, ogres, and werewolves, urban legends warn about hitchhikers, computer hackers, and terrorists. Instead of setting cautionary tales in castles, swamps, and haunted woods, urban legends warn about danger in lover's lanes, airplanes, and shopping malls.

I refer to cautionary tales about the Bible as *biblical urban legends* for at least three reasons:

- The first is that the phrase gets to the essence of what urban legends do. Urban legends might start with an element of truth, but they take on lives of their own as they are perpetuated. In the same way, Bible verses turned into biblical urban legends might start with an element of truth but they take on lives of their own as they are told and retold.

- The second reason is to call attention to our own era. When Bible verses become disconnected from their original story and social contexts, they take on meanings in our own time and place. This is when they become strange new creations.

- The most important reason to use the phrase is to make clear that Bible verses cut off from any

> connection to original context very quickly turn
> into cautionary tales rather than heroic stories.
> Biblical urban legends do what urban legends do.
> They create fear, anxiety, and confusion in the
> minds of believers as they warn against the
> dangers facing anyone who violates the rules.

I can think of no better description of so many of the contemporary stories told about Bible verses about money than biblical urban legend. The core of truth becomes false as it takes on a life of its own apart from the original context of the story. Biblical urban legends turn gospel stories into warnings about money based on the false assumption that the words of Jesus can be applied directly to a different time and place as if time and place don't matter.

Urban legends are not heroic. Both urban legends and biblical urban lessons exist to warn against lurking dangers. They do not teach heroism in the face of such dangers. They teach you to be afraid. Biblical urban legends never empower people because they produce fear, limitation, anxiety, and constriction.

The Story of the Rich Man as a Biblical Urban Legend

My candidate for the most damaging of all of the biblical urban legends about money is the story about the rich man who asked Jesus a question about eternal life. The story ends with words of Jesus about *a rich man, a camel, the eye of a needle,* and *the kingdom of God* or *kingdom of heaven.*

This one comment about a rich man and the kingdom of heaven is probably the single most misunderstood verse about money among all of the words of Jesus. It is my candidate for the Bible verse most likely to produce people who are afraid of becoming rich out of fear for their own salvation. My claim is that almost everything you have heard about these words is some sort of biblical urban legend.

How to Create a Biblical Urban Legend

One of the first ways to create a biblical urban legend is to do what the questioner did. He misquoted the verse and then created meaning out of the misquotation. In the process, he made his own biblical urban legend: "Jesus said that a rich man can't get into heaven." If you make the same assumption as the questioner—that the kingdom of heaven is the same as heaven—this is a very grim prognosis for rich people.

It's reasonable to assume that someone who goes to a seminar about creating a millionaire mindset about money would like to be rich. If this is true, the man who asked the question wanted to be rich, but believed that being rich was going to keep him out of heaven. The real source of his conflict was his own biblical urban legend: "Jesus said that a rich man can't get into heaven."

Loopholes for the Rich

If you are poor, you can celebrate that the rich will finally get what they deserve. You'll get into heaven. The rich won't. If however, you are already rich or you want to be rich, then the story becomes problematic. What do you do if you are a rich person or you want to be rich person? It's easy. You find ways to make the words mean something other than what they seem to mean. You need a biblical urban legend that takes a different tack. You need a *loophole*.

In the three biblical versions of the story, Jesus says that it's easier for a camel to go through the eye of a needle than for a rich man to enter the kingdom of heaven. This is bad news for a rich man. After all, what's the chance of a camel going through the eye of a needle?

The Eye of the Needle

A *literal* meaning of a word refers to its ordinary meaning. A literal meaning of the "eye of a needle" refers to the tiny hole of sewing needle. Since the literal meaning quite effectively keeps a rich man out of the kingdom of heaven— which most people equate with heaven—a classic biblical urban legend was born. It gives a rich man a loophole by turning a literal meaning into a metaphorical meaning. This loophole took the form of a gate in Jerusalem called *The Eye of the Needle Gate.*

As the story is told, this gate was so small that a camel could squeeze through, but only barely, and only if all the baggage was taken off the camel. Travelers to Jerusalem in the Victorian Era claimed that they had actually seen the Eye of the Needle Gate—and we can fairly assume that rich people were more likely to make such a trip than poor people.

As far as any archeologist or historian of Jerusalem can tell, there was never a gate in Jerusalem called The Eye of the Needle. The idea apparently goes back to a single source in the fifteenth century. Yet, a quick Google search will find entries confidently proclaiming that Jesus was "really" referring to this gate.

Threading a Needle with a Rope

Meanwhile, other efforts to explain what the words "really mean" claim that there is a translation problem. Instead of *camel*, this explanation claims that the word is supposed to be the Greek word for *rope*. Although putting a rope through the eye of a sewing needle might be an impossible challenge, even the biggest rope is smaller than the smallest camel. This solution requires a different needle with a bigger hole.

Usually, this type of explanation goes into great detail about the kind of needle used—that Matthew and Mark used the word for *sewing needle* while Luke used the word for *surgical needle*. This explanation increases the odds of the rich man squeezing into heaven.

When All Else Fails, Try Allegory

Whether preachers understand the eye of the needle as a real gate or a metaphorical one, this story about the eye of the needle has launched ten thousand sermon illustrations. It holds out the promise that you can get into heaven—even if you are rich—if you remove all of the baggage of pride and greed and envy. Now we are into the realm of allegories. Allegories make people, objects and actions within a story stand for abstract ideas. This is the biblical urban legend the speaker used when he asserted that Jesus was making an allegory about greed.

This isn't a complete list of all of the stories people have made up by taking the words of Jesus out of the original context of the three gospel narratives in which the story appears, but they are enough to make the point. The words of Jesus about the rich man produce a mother lode for biblical urban legends about money—all the while completing missing the intended point of the story.

The Liberating Remedy for Biblical Urban Legends

Why are all of these explanations biblical urban legends?:

- Not one of these explanations puts the stories into the context of the narrative.

- Not one adequately explains what the kingdom of heaven or kingdom of God means in the narrative.

- Not one explains what salvation means in the story itself.

- Not one puts the story into its social, historical, political, religious, and economic context.

As a result, every one of these biblical urban legends misses the point.

The only liberating remedy for a biblical urban legend is a method that first puts Bible verses into the context of the whole story and puts the whole story into the context of the society in which Jesus lived and taught. After figuring out what the story meant in its original story context, you are in a much better position to determine what it means for you in the economic context of the twenty-first century.

Part Two

Society

and

Stories

Chapter 4
Verses versus Verses

Time magazine ran a cover story with the provocative question: "Does God want you to be rich?" (September 18, 2006). The story itself follows the typical journalistic format of consulting proponents of two "camps": "the Prosperity Camp" and "the Social Justice Camp."

In separate boxes, David Van Biema and Jeff Chu include various Bible verses about wealth under the heading, "Verses vs. Verses." On one page, they cite five Bible verses under the heading, "It's God's Gift." On the opposite page, they cite five other Bible verses under the heading, "No, It's Not."

The fact that a national newsmagazine would even ask such a question on its cover demonstrates that "what the Bible says about money" is not just a religious matter. Biblical statements about money affect all of us, whether we are overtly religious or not, or even whether we are aware of it or not.

After raising the question, consulting the proponents, and laying out two sets of Bible verses, the authors end the article with a comment that makes being rich a spiritual matter:

> If God does want us to be rich in this life, no doubt
> it's this richness in spirit that he is most eager for us
> to acquire.

When authors resort to the words, "no doubt," to end an argument, it's a clear sign that they have no idea how to resolve the question.

Verses versus Verses

The Time article unintentionally demonstrates why this is so and even gives a name for the process: "verses vs. verses." *Verses versus verses* describes what often happens when Christians quote the Bible as the definitive authority on controversial issues. Discussion quickly hardens into opposing positions based on different Bible verses.

When people start with Bible verses, the tendency is to start with individual verses and then create some sort of universal law without analyzing the specific context of the material. The fundamental flaw in this tactic is a problem of logic. When people argue from the particular to the universal, it stands to reason that the universal depends on which particular you start with.

Choosing Different Verses

The Prosperity Camp and the Social Gospel Camp choose different verses to build a "Christian doctrine of money." The Prosperity Camp chooses verses emphasizing blessing. Their argument relies mostly on Old Testament verses, based on an understanding that wealth is a sign of God's blessing. The Social Gospel Camp chooses verses to make the case that Jesus preached against wealth and was concerned about social justice for the poor.

As long as people attempt to build *the* Christian doctrine of money by starting with Bible verses, consensus is impossible. Impasse between opposing camps is the inevitable result of verses versus verses.

A Method to Solve the Problem

Albert Einstein said that you cannot solve a problem with the mind that created it. With due credit to Einstein, I want to modify his statement to claim:

> You cannot solve a problem with the method that created it.

The purpose of this book is to demonstrate a method to get beyond the impasse of laying out two sets of Bible verses and leaving it up to you to decide which ones you will accept as relevant to your own financial life. In other words, the verses versus verses method created the problem. We need another method to solve it.

Context

The method is to put Bible verses into context. As a seminary student in my first preaching course, I learned an adage that has stayed with me ever since:

> A text without a context is a pretext.

Often, paying attention to the origin of a word gives insight into its meaning. In Latin, the word *text* refers to what is woven. A *pretext* is a fringe or covering that often obscures what is behind it. A *context* refers to weaving together. There is no better description of the inevitable result of *verses versus verses*. When a Bible verse is separated from its context, it becomes a pretext, obscuring what is behind it.

Every Bible verse has multiple contexts. A Bible verse is part of some sort of written document. The document was written in a particular language, at a particular time, in a particular place, in a particular social and economic environment, based on a particular theology. The Bible also developed over time. It has layers upon layers of text, language, historical, social, political, and theological contexts. Every single one of these particular factors is a distinct context. And so a Bible verse is not simply a discrete group of words. It is a group of words set of overlapping contexts.

What the Bible Meant

My focus on context comes from my own training as a biblical scholar. The technical word describing the primary task of biblical scholarship is *exegesis*—which means *to lead out of*. The goal of biblical scholarship is to delve deeply into these multilayered contexts to determine what the Bible *meant* in its own terms.

After I decided that I would write for a non-academic rather than an academic audience, I used to roam around the bookseller displays at the annual professional meetings of the American Academy of Religion and the Society of Biblical Literature. Publishers' booths were filled with hundreds of books written by brilliant scholars who devote their lives to the task of exegesis.

Why Biblical Scholars Leave Interpretation to Others

As I looked at the books, I knew that very little of this brilliant analysis gets translated into the churches and the public arena. The books are too scholarly, too filled with technical language, too opaque to address the *so what?* questions of ordinary people.

The books written for people in churches and the general public tend to written by people who are not biblical scholars. Although there are notable exceptions, the general tendency is for the work of biblical scholars to remain hidden away within the heady confines of academia.

Meanwhile, the Bible is interpreted for the general public and people in churches by theologians, pastors, and others who are not very well trained in the complexities and rigors of biblical exegesis. The situation would be something like having a highly trained doctor who devotes a lifetime to studying the brain but leaves neurosurgery to a second-year medical student.

A Division of Labor

The usual explanation for this situation goes back to the end of the eighteenth century and a German scholar, Johann Philipp Gabler. Gabler suggested a division of labor. Biblical scholars would do exegesis of the Bible, while theologians would do hermeneutics. *Hermeneutics* is a technical word to describe the process of interpretating the meaning of the Bible in the contemporary world.

In the middle of the twentieth century, Krister Stendahl crystallized the distinction into a memorable phrase. Biblical scholars would concentrate on exegesis—*what it meant*—and theologians would concentrate on hermeneutics—*what it means*.

Although the reality is not quite so stark, the overall tendency is that biblical scholars have operated for two hundred years with the idea that they are supposed to figure out "what it meant" and let others describe "what it means." The practical result is that what biblical scholars have to say about the Bible is seldom heard in public discussion. There are exceptions but the general tendency is for biblical scholars to write for other academics.

When I first began to read Greek and Hebrew as a seminary student, I had my first glimpses of how much my life had been affected by mistranslated, misinterpreted Bible verses. I began to recognize the enormous gap between what the scholars know and what the people in the churches learn. I began to see clearly how much I thought I knew about the Bible were texts without contexts—they were pretexts turned into biblical urban legends.

The Bible in Public

Public discussion of the Bible tends to become the province of people who are limited to reading English translations. They have very little understanding of the ancient world.

They are also unaware of the myriad complications involved in understanding what any of the ancient biblical material meant in its own contexts. This means that teaching "what the Bible says about money" often becomes the province of clergy and laypeople who are not deeply trained in biblical exegesis.

What Clergy Learn about the Bible in Seminary

I make that statement based on my own experience as a seminary student and as a teacher in theological seminaries. I taught biblical studies to future pastors, priests, and ministers, both in my own classes and as a teaching assistant during my graduate work.

The courses the students took depended on the ordination requirements of their own church denominations. This means that some seminary students study both Greek and Hebrew, some study only Greek, and some study neither language. Even seminarians required to study Greek and Hebrew take only a year of each language. Many treat the languages simply as hoops to jump through to fulfill ordination requirements.

I heard many students declare that their pastors or ministers claimed they never used the biblical languages they were required to study in seminary. This meant that many of my students began seminary with the idea that they would again never look at Hebrew or Greek after they passed their ordination exams.

Most seminary students take no more than three or four Bible courses, if that. There are simply too many other classes in such topics as ministry, theology, ethics, preaching, church history, pastoral counseling, worship, and courses such as liturgical dance to take many biblical studies courses.

In addition, seminary students often spend hours each week working in churches as trainees and interns. Their work schedules also included several hours on Sunday.

One of my own frustrations as a teacher of seminary students was that they were so busy working in churches and participating in worship services that they had little time left over for classes and coursework. That was especially true during Christmas and Easter seasons. Some of my students explained that they were required to participate in ten-to-twelve worship services during Holy Week and couldn't possibly do homework.

Throughout the school year, week after week, there was always something going on in the churches that pulled them away from coursework. Even the most diligent students had great difficulty keeping up with the dual demands of coursework and churchwork. The practical result is that few seminary students are very well trained in biblical exegesis.

Clergy and Bible Study

When these students become clergy, they put in sixty-to-eighty hour workweeks, deeply involved with pastoral care, administration, counseling, and worship. While some clergy are deeply committed to rigorous Bible study, most clergy don't have time to do in-depth Bible study even if they want to do it.

The result is that many of the sermons on Bible verses that people hear in church are preached by people who are both over-worked and under-trained in biblical exegesis—*what it meant*. They simply don't have the time or training to do careful translations based on social, historical, literary, and linguistic study.

At the same time, clergy do hermeneutics—*what it means*—on a daily basis. They teach, preach, and counsel in very practical ways in real life situations.

Contrary to the stereotypes of clergy in movies and TV shows, the vast majority of clergy are neither corrupt nor hopelessly naïve. Most of the clergy I have known deal on a daily basis with life, death, conflict, and anguish. People ask their pastors, ministers, and priests for biblical answers to the most difficult human questions. Yet, many of the clergy can do little more than quote Bible verses out of context to provide answers. As a result, even the most well-meaning, dedicated, compassionate clergy often unintentionally perpetuate biblical urban legends.

What It Meant Comes before What It Means

My method is based on my own compelling belief that the only way to prevent pretexts and biblical urban legends is to put exegesis before hermeneutics. *What it meant* must precede *what it means*.

In this book, I focus on two essential contexts that often get left out when people do hermeneutics without exegesis—when they proclaim what it means without first attempting to determine what it meant.

Social Context

The first is the context of *society*. Any time a person from the twenty-first century reads the Bible, two relevant social contexts are involved. The first is the social context of the twenty-first century itself. The second is the social context of the ancient world. The challenge is to realize how often our own social contexts blind us to the realities of the social contexts of the ancient world.

Story Context

The second is the context of *story*. The New Testament contains four distinct narratives about Jesus called gospels—the Gospels of Matthew, Mark, Luke, and John.

Each has its unique differences and each has similarities with the others, but the relevant point is that each is a distinct type of story called a *gospel*. The gospel genre is directly related to the meaning of these stories.

What It Means in American Context

Throughout, my focus is on what all of this means in the context of the United States. I make no effort to address what any of this means in other contemporary societies. I am profoundly aware that economic issues in the twenty-first century are never simply local because of our globally interconnected economic systems. However, I am also profoundly aware that American society is the only society I know from the inside out. Therefore, I write as an American about what I know about the use and abuse of Bible verses about money in the United States. If this is not your own social context, I invite you to consider what all of this means for you wherever you are in the world.

Does Jesus Want You to Be Broke?

Time Magazine asked the question: "Does God want you to be rich?" This book asks an even more provocative question: *Does Jesus want you to be broke?* Maybe the term *broke* is a bit harsh. I could be more polite by using other terms. Financially challenged. Struggling to make ends meet. Scraping by. However, the impolite word *broke* gets to the heart of the matter.

What better word than *broke* to describe someone who reaches the age of sixty-five without enough money to be financially independent and must depend upon meager Social Security and Medicare payments that don't cover expenses?

What better word than *broke* to describe people who work for a lifetime, thinking that they will retire comfortably with a pension, only to discover that former employers can wipe out pensions with one corporate resolution, restructure the corporation, and leave the stockholders richer and the hapless employees wondering whatever happened to obligation, responsibility, loyalty, honesty, and respect?

What about the middle class, which is getting squeezed by higher mortgages, rising health costs, and increasing personal debt from interest rates on credit cards that have reached usurious levels? Many people are one or two paychecks away from financial trouble. A lost job or an illness can lead to financial ruin.

Especially now, in tough economic times, what about people on the bottom who cannot get out from under? What about people who have lost their jobs and their houses? What about people who work for low wages but cannot pay their bills? What about people who cannot pay their mortgages? What better word to describe all of this than broke?

Broken Spirits

As a metaphor, the word *broke* also carries another connotation besides being out of money. It evokes the notion of being broken, the way horses are *broken* when they are taught to submit to the will of the rider.

Many of us are broke, not just because we have challenges with money, but because somewhere along the line, our spirits were broken by religious education filled with *Constraining Bible* verses claiming that it was bad to be rich and good to be poor. It's not just about money. It's about power and the freedom to make your own choices, including the power to take control of your finances.

Broke among Millionaires

Meanwhile, while many people are broke or vulnerable to becoming broke, other people in our society are making extraordinary amounts of money. There are more and more millionaires and even some billionaires. A tiny percentage of people make billions while millions more go broke.

My question is: Does Jesus have anything to do with creating an economic system in which so many people go broke in the richest society on earth?

Religion in the United States of America

The United States of America is a pluralistic society, comprising people from every nation on Planet Earth. The population includes people of every religion and no religion. Officially, the Constitution of the United States requires the separation of church and state. Officially, it offers freedom of religion and freedom from religion.

In reality, the Christian roots of the United States are extremely deep and the majority of the population identify themselves as Christian. In its March 2007 poll, Newsweek claims that eighty-two percent of Americans identify themselves as Christian. In addition, many people who no longer identify themselves as Christian grew up Christian and remain deeply influenced by Christian beliefs about money. In a society shaped by Christian beliefs from the beginning and still predominantly Christian, many people go broke. Is this a coincidence?

The Wealthiest One-to-Three Percent

It's too simplistic to draw a direct line between Christian beliefs and a population in which many people teeter on the edge of going broke. Most societies of the world demonstrate the same disparity. One-to-three percent of the population controls the lion's share of the wealth.

What is especially remarkable is that this percentage has been characteristic of agrarian societies, industrial economies, and modern capitalist economies, both in the past and in the contemporary world.

So, what's the issue? The real issue is that a country that is predominantly Christian has the same money issues as other societies. A few people are very, very rich, a significant percentage of people are very, very poor, and many others struggle constantly to have enough money.

Does Jesus Want You to Be Poor?

The authors of the Time Magazine article ask: Does God want you to be rich? I ask a different question: Does the Jesus of the Christian gospels want to maintain the status quo in which a few people are very rich and most people are either very poor or constantly struggling for money? The concise question is: Does Jesus want you to be poor?

This leads to my fundamental exegetical question: Has the Christian church correctly understood what Jesus meant to say about money in a society divided between rich and poor? As a matter of logical possibilities, the options are:

Jesus wants everyone to be rich.

Jesus wants no one to be rich.

Jesus wants everyone to be poor.

Jesus wants no one to be poor.

Jesus wants some people to be rich and some people to be poor.

How Christian Education Keeps Many People Broke

My premise is that Christian education about money based on isolated Bible verses has the effect of keeping many people broke or teetering on the edge of being broke. Much When Christian teaching extracts Bible verses out of context, with little attention to the context of the story or the context of the society, the words of Jesus become biblical urban legends. Without story and without context, these biblical urban legends keep many believers broke in both senses of the word—without money and without power.

How Does Faith Matter?

As a biblical scholar, committed to putting exegesis before hermeneutics, I intend to leave faith out of the discussion. Nothing in this book challenges Christian belief in Jesus as the Son of God. And nothing in this book argues for Christian belief in the Jesus as the Son of God.

Exegesis is not a matter of faith. It is a matter of making a commitment to read the Bible on its own terms. Whatever you believe about Jesus and whatever I believe about Jesus do not change the social realities of ancient Palestine and the contemporary world and they do not change the narratives themselves. The narratives of Jesus are what they are. The society of Jesus was what it was. The society in which we live is what it is.

My goal is to give you a glimpse of the liberating insights of biblical scholarship, so that you can experience what I first began to realize as a seminary student. I realized that most of what I learned in Sunday School, Bible studies, and church had completely missed the point and created unjustified fear and limitation. It was *Constraining Bible* rather than *Liberating Bible*.

Faith becomes an issue for hermeneutics. After you make an effort to read the gospels stories of Jesus on their own terms, in their own contexts, your interpretative task is to decide what it all means to you and to American society in an economically interconnected world in the twenty-first century.

Chapter 5
Follow the Money

Any story is a product of its own social context. In the brief encounter between the questioner at the seminar who was sure that a rich man could not get into heaven and the speaker who claimed that the verse in question was a caution against being greedy, what we see is that both comments treat Jesus' words to the rich man about money as a moralistic matter applying to an individual. In the process, both miss the fundamental reality that money is never simply a personal matter.

Follow the Money as the Guiding Principle

Follow the money was the guiding principle that Robert Woodward and Carl Bernstein used as investigative reporters to undercover the real story behind the infamous Watergate burglary and subsequent cover-up during the Nixon administration. The same *follow the money* principle also uncovers the real story behind the gospel narratives. Money is the unifying foundation of the Gospels of Matthew, Mark, and Luke. The essence of these three gospel stories is Jesus' single-minded condemnation of an unjust economic system.

The Big Mushroom Lying beneath the Gospel Stories

My question is: If the gospel narratives are primarily about Jesus' condemnation of an unjust economic system, why do people treat the references to money as matters of personal morality?

The best way to answer this question is with a metaphor about a mushroom. Experts claim that the largest living organism on earth is a gigantic *honey mushroom* in eastern Oregon. This particular fungus covers twenty-two hundred acres, stretches more than three and a half miles across and covers more ground than sixteen hundred football fields.

The particular relevance of this mushroom as a metaphor for money in the gospel narratives is that most of this giant fungus lies three feet beneath the surface. The small mushrooms that pop to the surface are connected to the giant unified mushroom underground. If you see only the surface, all you can see are individual mushrooms. When you go beneath the surface, you discover that the surface mushrooms emerge from a single source.

The few explicit comments Jesus makes about money in the gospel narratives are simply surface mushrooms. All are connected to the larger mushroom beneath the surface. The underground mushroom is a metaphor for an advanced agrarian economic system in which wealth was derived from the land. Every comment about money grows out of its connection to the agrarian economic system hidden beneath the surface.

Why Do We Miss the Big Money Mushroom?

The question remains: Why do so many Bible readers see the surface money mushrooms with no awareness of the huge money mushroom beneath the narrative? Why do so many readers treat money as an occasional topic, without recognizing that the economic system shapes the entire story?

Filter One: Verses Versus Verses

The primary reason is that contemporary American Bible readers read the Bible through powerful filters. The first filter is the *verses versus verses* method when people make meaning from discrete Bible verses instead of entire narratives. This method of reading pieces of the story without putting the pieces into the context of the whole narrative remains the single biggest obstacle to understanding the underlying context that produced the narratives.

Filter Two: Separation of Religion from Politics

A second powerful filter is separation of religion from government. Americans live in a political system that officially separates church and state. The United States of America is deeply rooted in Christian belief. However, the Founding Fathers created a Constitution based on the radical idea that religion can and should be separated from government. They took great care to separate church and state as a fundamental tenet of American society.

In reality, the line between church and state is often blurred, particularly in recent years. However, this constitutional intention to separate religion from government has significant implications when we look at what Jesus said about money.

Filter Three: The Economic System

The third filter concerns the economic system itself. In any economic system, money is never just a matter for an individual because money is the reason why there are social classes. Money separates people into *the haves* and *the have-nots*, *the ins* and *the outs*. Money creates political power. Money also creates religious power. People tend to read the stories of Jesus about money without seeing the dramatic differences between the economic systems of first century Palestine and twenty-first century America.

Saving Souls or Saving Society

A strong tradition exists within certain aspects of American Christianity to treat religion and government as two separate spheres with no inherent connection between them. This is especially true in some of the Protestant churches that are most committed to the authority of scripture. This tendency has created a division of labor: the church saves souls and lets the government take care of the society.

More recently, other Christians have been involved in concerted political action to remove any separation between church and state. Their purpose is to create a nation ruled by "biblical law."

In contrast to these two tendencies, some churches are deeply involved in economic and political issues as part of their commitment to social justice. This is the fundamental stance of the "Social Gospel Camp" identified in the Time Magazine article.

However, despite the political efforts of some Christian groups to "recreate a Christian nation" and the long-standing commitment to social justice of other Christian groups, a significant portion of American Christianity has concentrated on personal salvation without concerning itself very much with inequities in the structure of the society.

Individualism

The tendency to separate religion from politics also tends to separate the person from the society. This leads to individualism and a focus on an individual relationship with God. From this perspective, the Bible then becomes a manual of personal salvation without much concern for the place of the person in the society. From this perspective, the true focus of religion is the salvation of individuals rather than the salvation of a society.

With this perspective, the Bible then becomes about *me*. What is *my* relationship with God? What must *I* do to be saved? How must *I* act so that *I* will get to heaven? All of these questions are expressed in personal terms.

Both of the comments at the seminar between the man who asked about the rich man and getting into heaven and the speaker who responded with a comment about greed focus on the meaning of the words for an individual. Neither one goes beyond the individual to place both the question and the answer into either the social context of ancient Palestine or the social context of contemporary America. (When we return to the story about the rich man in Chapter 17, we'll see that he too was thinking only about his own salvation rather than his place in the economic system.)

Advanced Agrarian Society

Israel, in first century Palestine, was an *advanced agrarian society*. Gerhard Lenski, in *Power and Privilege*, pictures the relationship of the various classes in an agrarian society. Imagine a plumber's plunger with a very short handle. At the very top of the plunger, a tiny percentage of the population controlled the land. About one percent of the population had wealth, power, and privilege. They also created and used wealth in ways that impoverished most of the population. Everyone else fit somewhere into the broad base of the plunger. A middle class didn't exist. This economic system, with its tremendous disparity of wealth, is the huge mushroom underneath the surface of the narrative.

In an agrarian society, wealth is based on land. In a capitalist society, such as the United States, wealth is based on money itself—capital. This difference is extremely significant for reading the gospel stories.

When God Owns the Land

In contemporary American society, anyone can own land. Owning your own home and your own land has always been the fundamental promise of the American Dream. The lure of this dream fueled the massive boom in real estate investing as the fastest route to creating wealth—a boom that abruptly turned into financial ruin for many.

However, no one could have made money in ancient Palestine as a real estate investor because the land was not for sale. Land ownership in an agrarian society was based on a complicated religious and political ideology. The land was not for sale for the simple reason that only God owned the land.

Israel shared this understanding of the ownership of land with every other society of the Ancient Near East. They all agreed that the land belonged to the local god. The only dispute among different societies was which god owned a particular portion of the land.

One of the blessings provided to human beings by the gods was the use of the land. Human beings could live on the land, raising crops and tending animals, with the clear understanding that the land belonged to the god. In exchange for allowing people to live on the land and grow food, the gods expected to be acknowledged as the owners of the land through offerings of produce and sacrifices of animals. (Think of the whole system of sacrifices and offerings as a way to pay rent for the use of the land.)

Israel shared the same land ideology. The God of Israel owned the land. The people paid "rent" for the privilege of living on the land by offering both animals and produce at the temple. The offerings acknowledged that God owned the land.

Religion Is Always Political

So far, this is a religious ideology about ownership of the land, but religious ideology is always political. In this ideological system, God *owned* the land, but the kings *ruled* it. They were regents for the real landowner, God.

As the human agent for God, the king controlled the land—all of the land—except for the small portion of land set aside for the temple. Although the ideology claimed that the kings didn't *own* the land, the kings could decide how to *use* the land. Whatever the theological foundation of land ownership, by every practical standard, the kings acted as sovereign land owners. The king gave estates to his supporters from the urban elite social class. This land-controlling elite class could subject the peasant farmers to any demands they wished.

Property Rights

This brings us to one of the biggest differences between the way we understand property rights and the way agrarian societies understood property rights. We tend to think of property as *things*. Agrarian rulers thought of property as *rights*. So the king didn't have to own the land to have rights to it. In an agrarian society, the king had property rights to *all* of the land.

Even when the peasant farmers *owned the land* itself, the king and the ruling class *owned the rights* to the land. The king controlled all agriculture. The government decided what was grown, how much was grown, how much farmers could get paid for the crops, and demanded payment of taxes. In addition, peasant farmers were required to turn over a portion of their crops to the elite class.

Rent and Taxes in Advanced Agrarian Societies

If you think you are over-taxed, consider the situation of a peasant in an advanced agrarian society. In addition to the proprietary claims by the king, peasants owed rent to the urban elite who owned the property rights to the peasants' land. The peasants also owed other taxes, including taxes to the temple. As a result, peasants paid as much as four-fifths of what they produced to the ruling class. Peasant farmers living on the land suffered great poverty while a tiny elite class controlled most of the wealth.

Even then, the peasants who could stay on their family land were the fortunate ones. Peasant farmers who could not pay the rents and taxes lost their land and became part of the large landless underclass. This included sons who could not inherit the family land because the land passed to the oldest son. Younger sons became landless artisans and craftsmen.

[Just as an aside, sometimes you will read that Jesus was a member of the middle-class because he was a carpenter—a skilled artisan. Such claims don't take seriously enough the economic reality of an agrarian society—which had no "middle class"—or the social status of artisans, who were usually landless.]

The Degraded and the Expendable

In addition to the large peasant class, I'll mention two additional groups—the *degraded* and the *expendables*. The degraded ones did work that was either unskilled or considered ritually unclean. The expendables were nonproductive people, such as beggars, lepers, and thieves.

[And in another aside, few people at Christmas Eve services understand the truly radical nature of the appearance of an angel to shepherds:

And in that region there were shepherds out in the field, keeping watch over their flock by night. And an angel of the Lord appeared to them, and the glory of the Lord shone around them, and they were filled with fear. And the angel said to them, "Be not afraid; for behold, I bring you good news of a great joy which will come to all the people; for to you is born this day in the city of David a Savior, who is Christ the Lord (Luke 2:8-11, Revised Standard Version).

Because shepherds tended to animals, they were engaged in a profession that was considered ritually unclean. The shepherds would not have been welcome at the temple that night because of their unclean status. The announcement to the shepherds is simply one more indication that the good news of the kingdom of God is for the outcasts, the unclean, and the expendables.]

So, even though the religious ideology claimed that God was the true owner of the land, by every earthly standard, the king and rest of the ruling class with property rights to the land acted as if they owned the land to the great detriment of the peasant landowners.

Temples in an Advanced Agrarian Society

Temples were part of this ideological system about ownership of the land. Temples in ancient societies served several functions. Temples were never simply religious. A temple is first of all the house of the god. The priests were house servants who tended to the god's house.

Since the god owned the land, the temple also served as the tax collector. When people took their offerings and sacrifices to the temples, they were paying a form of rent that was collected and administered by the temple, which was in turn maintained by the monarchy.

No Separation of Religion and Politics

Already, we can see that the king, the temple, and the land were all part of the same ideological package. Any effort to separate religion and government into separate spheres completely misses the fundamental interconnection between religion, government, and land.

Under this ideological system, the society was divided into the *haves* and the *have nots*. There were very few *haves*. In such a system, wealth was considered a sign of God's blessing. Clearly, the most blessed was the king.

This ideology would never have treated religion as a separate entity from government and would never have treated the individual as separate from that individual's social class.

Roman Occupation

One last fact before moving on is that Palestine in the first century was under the domination of the Roman Empire. It was an occupied territory and the empire and the local procurator demanded their share of taxes and tributes, which added to the economic oppression of the population.

The Wealth Gap in the Gospels

The essential point is that Jesus lived in a society of extreme poverty for most of the population. The society was ruled by a religious and political system that had no reason to care about the wellbeing of the majority of the people.

The huge gap in wealth—money—between the rich and the rest of the population motivates the gospels. This is the mushroom lying beneath the surface.

Each of the three synoptic gospels—Matthew, Mark, and Luke—is about this huge gap in wealth. Economic reality motivates all three of the stories as Jesus sets out to confront an unjust society, with its underlying ideology that wealth for the very rich was a sign of God's blessing.

Part Three

Stories

of

The Outlaw Hero

Chapter 6
Reclaiming the Gospels as Stories

The Four Gospels Are Stories

The four gospels of the New Testament—Matthew, Mark, Luke, and John—are stories about a man named Jesus. They have biographical elements but they are not biographies. The narratives themselves are made up of stories about his life and death. They tell stories about his teaching, his relationship with his disciples, confrontations with enemies, public teaching, healing, exorcisms, his arrest and trial, his death and resurrection, and appearances to his disciples after resurrection.

Stories must be as basic to human life as the need to breathe. Listen to people talk about their lives. People talk in stories. "I did this and that happened. Then I did that and that happened. Then something else happened." This is why the news comes in the form of news stories. Movies tell stories. Books tell stories. We read stories to our children. Without stories, life would be a series of random events. Stories turn events in narratives.

When people take the words of Jesus out of the story and treat them as adages, as discrete sayings, as words of wisdom, they miss the essential characteristic of the four gospels. All four gospels are stories about a storyteller.

Punchlines and Biblical Urban Legends

Here's a way to think about Bible verses about money. Compare them to the punchline of a joke. A great joke teller sets up the punchline by telling a story. The story leads to the punchline. On contrast, a bad joketeller bungles a joke, usually by giving the punchline without setting up the story. Without a story, there is no joke.

When story punchlines get disconnected from their original stories, they don't stay disconnected very long. A story needs a punchline and a punchline needs a story. Very soon, the disconnected punchline attracts another story.

That was the basic problem for the man at the seminar who asked about the words of Jesus about the rich man and the kingdom of heaven. He had a punchline and lost the original story. As a result, he created a new story. Then the punchline of the original story into the punchline of a new story.

Since the questioner at the seminar had only a punchline, he created meaning by making up another story along the lines of:

> Jesus said that a rich man can't get into heaven. I would really like to be rich. But if I'm rich, I won't get into heaven. Therefore, I'd better not be rich, because I want to be sure that I'll get into heaven.

Biblical urban legends are the result of extracting the punchline from a biblical story and then creating another story. The new story changes the point of the original story.

The Gospel as a Unique Type of Story

Although there are other stories about Jesus in the New Testament, Matthew, Mark, Luke, and John are a unique type of story called a *gospel*. It seems that the writer of the Gospel of Mark created a new story genre to tell his story about Jesus. The essence of the gospel genre is its name, *euaggelion*. The word combines the Greek words meaning *good* (*eu*) and *message*. Message is derived from the Greek word for *angel*. (The *gg* is pronounced as if it were *ng*—

euangelion.) In the Bible, angels are messengers. The word *gospel* means *good news*.

Good News

The word *gospel* originated as a military term. In an era when the only way to get news was to hear it from a messenger, *euaggelion* was a message about victory in battle. The messenger arrived with the proclamation of good news: "The war is over. The enemy is defeated. We won." That is why it is good news.

As a first principle of understanding the money sayings of Jesus in the New Testament, we need to take seriously that Mark created a new genre to tell the story of Jesus. He didn't call it a history, a biography, a fable, a fairy tale, an allegory, or another of dozens of other possible types of stories. Mark invented the gospel genre—a story written to proclaim the good news of victory over an enemy.

The Hero's Journey

The essential point is that the New Testament gospels are stories. They are not sourcebooks of theological doctrine. As stories, they are all examples of a hero's journey. In 1949, Joseph Campbell published *The Hero with a Thousand Faces*. He gave a name to the most basic type of story told throughout human history in most cultures of the earth. Campbell's outline of the hero's journey has become the story structure of many movies, including the biggest blockbuster movies.

The critical motivation of the hero's journey is that the hero undertakes a task to solve a problem that threatens the wellbeing of the hero's world. To do this, the hero must defeat the chief adversary at the location of the adversary's greatest power.

Campbell identified various stages the hero undergoes as a three-act structure: beginning, middle, and end. The hero's journey is a story with three acts.

First Act

In the first act, the hero leaves the hero's familiar world to solve a problem. The hero is called out of the ordinary world by some challenge, which the hero may be reluctant to accept. A hero often has a mentor who provides the hero with some essential gift for the journey.

Second Act

In the second act, the hero encounters obstacle after obstacle, making friends and enemies along the way. The journey is full of challenges and trials. The journey includes the central *ordeal* of the journey, represented as entry into the *inmost cave*. This is when the hero faces death. The second act ends when it looks as if all is lost.

Third Act

In the third act, the hero must meet the chief adversary in one climactic struggle to accomplish the purpose of the journey. The triumphant hero accomplishes the great task and returns home with an *elixir*. The elixir is a great gift for the people of the hero's ordinary world.

The Hero's Journey in Movies

In the original *Star Wars* movies, Luke Skywalker follows the steps of the hero's journey in his battle against the Empire. Obi-Wan Kenobi is the mentor who gives Luke the light saber. Luke gathers his allies and makes enemies. He undergoes powerful ordeals including confrontations and near-death experiences before his confrontational battles with Darth Vader. In his hero's journey, Luke is one of the Jedi knights who destroy the empire.

Titanic was a blockbuster movie that followed the hero's journey form. In this case, the hero was Rose, a young woman who was called out of her ordinary life into a new life of adventure.

The *Harry Potter* books and the movies made from them are classic hero's journeys. Young Harry is called out of his ordinary muggle world into the special wizard world of Hogwarts where he must eventually confront the evil Lord Voldemort.

The *Lord of the Rings* books and movies are also three parts of a hero's journey. The hobbit Frodo saves Middle Earth by throwing the ring of power into Mount Doom to destroy the power of the evil Lord Sauron.

Each of these stories follows the classic hero's journey formula. One of the reasons they are so wildly popular is because the hero's journey represents an ordinary person who becomes extraordinary by resolving to solve a threatening problem for the benefit of others.

The Difference between Gospels and Biblical Urban Legends

What difference does it make to read the gospel accounts of Jesus as hero's journeys? The defining characteristic of a hero is the choice to take action to solve a problem in the hero's world. A hero's journey is not easy. It's full of obstacles and hindrances in which the hero perseveres to solve the problem. In the process, the hero becomes much more resourceful, persistent, skillful, and powerful.

Powerless

Compare a hero's journey with a biblical urban legend. It's the difference between power and powerlessness. The basic characteristic of biblical urban legends is fear leading to powerlessness. Often, Christian education teaches people the opposite of heroism. It teaches powerlessness.

One of the most vivid examples I know is a sermon preached by a retired bishop in a San Francisco church. The bishop had the shape of a fire hydrant and a basso profundo voice that was so loud it sounded like a boom box at full volume.

Jonah the Reluctant Hero

He told the very strange story of Jonah. Jonah was called by God to go to Nineveh to announce God's judgment against the city. In a hero's journey, this was Jonah's call to adventure. But Jonah was an extremely reluctant hero. He immediately headed in the opposite direction. He boarded a ship to take him as far away from Nineveh as possible.

However, God chased him down. God caused a storm to come up that threatened the ship. The frantic crew drew lots. They determined that their lives were in danger because of Jonah. Jonah told them to throw him overboard so that the storm would stop.

Then God sent a "great fish" to swallow Jonah. This is real hero's journey stuff here. This is Jonah's *ordeal* when he enters the *inmost cave*. In this case, the inmost cave is the belly of a great fish. Jonah undergoes his own ritual death. After three days and three nights, Jonah prays for salvation. Then God causes the fish to spit Jonah out onto dry land.

Then God again tells Jonah to announce God's judgment against Nineveh. This time, Jonah obeys. He goes to Nineveh and does what God commanded him to do. There's more to Jonah's story than this but the ending is not relevant to the point of the preacher's sermon: "It doesn't matter what you want. If God wants you to do it, God will make you do it."

By the time the preacher bellowed those words, the basso profundo was so loud that the little glass pendants in the chandeliers overhead were clanging against each other. I could feel the congregation shrinking. The whole sermon was overpowering, overwhelming, frightening. It was a verbal assault by a bullying preacher about a bullying god. That sermon demonstrated the essence of *Constraining Bible*.

When God Becomes the Godfather

That bellowed sermon was an extreme example, but Christian education about Jesus often makes the same point even if the volume is softer. God becomes the Godfather who makes Jesus an offer he cannot refuse. Jesus does what he does because he has no choice.

When biblical verses are extracted from these gospel narratives and turned into biblical urban legends, they do not become hero's stories that empower believers to act heroically. They become stories to shrink by.

In contrast to the bullying preacher's claim that God forced Jonah do what he didn't want to do, in the New Testament gospel stories, Jesus chooses to accept his call to be a hero. His hero's journey concerns the use and abuse of economic, political, and religious power in his society.

This is the essential difference between a gospel story and a biblical urban legend. A gospel story proclaims victory over an enemy. A biblical urban legend warns of danger. The most significant difference is the reaction of the reader or hearer.

Biblical urban legends about the words of Jesus about money turn Gospel Good News into constraining stories about money. What is good news about the notion that a rich man won't get into heaven? What is good news about the idea that you can be rich as long as you are not greedy? Where is the idea of victory over an enemy?

This is the biggest problem with biblical urban legends. It's not just that the words are taken out of context and turned into other stories. Biblical urban legends have lost the notion of gospel and the notion of victory over an enemy. You can usually recognize a biblical urban legend by the way you feel when you hear it. If it leaves you afraid, cautious, anxious, worried, and fearful, it's a fairly strong probability that you have encountered a biblical urban legend rather than a gospel story.

Four Stories Not Just One

It's also important to take seriously that there are four gospel stories. Why are there four? They were written by different authors, addressed to different audiences, and had difference purposes. However, the tendency in the Christian church is to treat the Bible as one unified story and to ignore the differences between these four gospel stories.

Chapter 7
Hero's Journeys of the Kingdom

The Synoptic Gospels

The four gospels about Jesus are Matthew, Mark, Luke, and John. The gospels of Matthew, Mark, and Luke are called the synoptic gospels because they are obviously related. *Synoptic* comes from *syn* (*with*) and *optikos* (from the word for *vision*). It means *seeing the whole together*.

The majority consensus of biblical scholarship is that Mark was written first. Then Matthew and Luke used Mark as the foundation of their narratives. Matthew and Luke had common source material (*Q*) that Mark did not have. And finally, each writer had unique source material.

The Kingdom of God

The central idea of the three synoptic gospels is the *kingdom of God*. In each story, Jesus is identified as the anointed one who proclaims that the kingdom of God is near.

The Gospel of John was apparently written without drawing on the synoptic gospels. Also, the kingdom of God is not the central idea of the Gospel of John. For these reasons, I'm going leave John aside and concentrate only the hero's journey of Jesus in Matthew, Mark, and Luke.

While Matthew, Mark, and Luke follow the same basic outline of the story, these three narratives have significant differences. Each is written for a different audience, to accomplish a different purpose, in response to some specific situation.

When Were the Gospels Written?

Although scholars disagree about when these gospels were written, most date them sometime during the period between 70 and 100 A.D.

Most scholars date Mark to the period around the destruction of the temple in Jerusalem in 70 A.D. This places the Gospel of Mark at least thirty-five years after the death of Jesus. The situation that motivated Mark to write the gospel was the Jewish Revolt against Rome. The revolt started in 66 A.D. and spread throughout the region in widespread rebellion. In its effort to smash the rebellion, Roman troops laid siege to Jerusalem. In 70 A.D., the Romans entered Jerusalem. They looted the temple of its treasures, including the Ark of the Covenant in the Holy of Holies—the same Ark of the Covenant that was the subject of the first Indiana Jones movie, *The Raiders of the Lost Ark*. Then they burned the temple to the ground. They also raped, robbed, or massacred the thousands of people who had survived famine during the long siege.

September 11, 2001

To understand the impact of this event, consider the trauma of the terrorist attacks on September 11, 2001. The World Trade Center and the Pentagon were chosen as targets because they were the most visible symbols of commerce and military power in the United States. Whether the intended target of the plane that crashed in Pennsylvania was the White House or the Congress, both are iconic symbols of the locus of political power. 9/11 has become a shorthand way to refer to a profoundly traumatic event in American shared national consciousness.

The destruction of the temple in Jerusalem produced that kind of trauma in the consciousness of the people of Israel. The temple was the ancient equivalent of the

Federal Reserve, the Internal Revenue Service, the Congress, and the Supreme Court in one location. Although it was not the equivalent of the White House—since the king had his own palace—the temple gave authority to the monarchy because it recognized the king as God's anointed one. In other words, the destruction of the temple was a devastating assault on the heart of power and identity of Israel.

The Gospel of Mark

The Gospel of Mark was written in response to this trauma. It was most likely addressed to Jewish Christians who had fled from Israel to Syria. The trauma also accounts for the emotional tone and urgency of his writing. Mark has to address a single question: What is God going to do about this assault?

For Mark, the answer is that Jesus Christ is going to return to initiate the kingdom of God in full power on earth. You can make a strong case that Mark expected that Jesus Christ would return in Mark's lifetime.

The Gospel of Matthew

The Gospel of Matthew was written ten-to-twenty years later. Matthew wrote it for Jews who had become Christians. Matthew's story is full of references to the Hebrew scriptures. Matthew makes the case that Jesus came to fulfill the Law of Moses. Matthew lays out the story in a five-part structure. The five-part structure is modeled on the five books of the Torah (Genesis, Exodus, Leviticus, Numbers, and Deuteronomy). After each of the five teaching sections, Matthew includes a section showing Jesus in action.

The Gospel of Luke

The Gospel of Luke was also written ten-to-twenty years after Mark. Luke wrote his story for Gentiles who had become Christians. Since Luke was not writing for people familiar with the Hebrew scriptures, Luke does not need to make the case that that Jesus is the fulfillment of the Law. Luke has a different persuasive task. He has to explain why the teachings of a Jew are relevant to Gentiles. He also has to explain why the promise of salvation also applies to Gentiles.

Why the Stories Are Different

These differences in audience and intention explain many differences between these three gospels. To give just one example, Mark is looking forward rather than backwards. He doesn't bother with the genealogy of Jesus. Since he is writing for Jews who have become Christian, Matthew takes the genealogy of Jesus back to David and Abraham, the "Father of the Jews." [Actually, the genealogy in Matthew raises questions about the genealogy of Jesus, which are discussed in *Your True Self Identity*.] In contrast, Luke takes the genealogy back to Adam because the Gentile people he is addressing have no direct connection to Abraham, the Father of the Jews. Luke connects Jesus to Adam, the father of all human beings.

The Kingdom of God

Despite these differences, the core concept driving all three of these stories is the *kingdom of God*. The fact that Matthew almost always used *kingdom of heaven* and Mark and Luke used the *kingdom of God* is a clue that the phrase is loaded with meaning. The scholar's way is to investigate all of the ways that the phrase was used in any context at any time—Hebrew scriptures, intertestamental writings, early Christian writings, and rabbinic writing. This means that studying the concept of the kingdom of God feels something like plunging into a swamp. The farther in you go, the deeper it gets, and the more bogged down you become.

My goal is to make it simple without being simplistic. The essential idea is that kingdom of God refers to the rule of God on earth.

Chapter 8
Jesus the Outlaw Hero

The Outlaw Archetype

In addition to the basic story structure of the hero's journey, a hero is what Carl Jung called an *archetype*. An archetype is an *ideal form*. The hero is an archetype of the *warrior* who triumphs over whatever threatens the hero's ordinary world.

One type of hero is the archetypal *outlaw* who challenges lawful authority. Whether someone is regarded as a hero or an outlaw is often a matter of perspective. A hero is regarded as an outlaw by those who are in power and a hero by those oppressed by the powerful. This is why the hero and the outlaw are often the same person.

Many of the most popular stories are outlaw stories. The outlaw hero seeks radical freedom from the power structure. The power structure regards the outlaw hero as a threat to its existence.

Outlaw Heroes

In *Star Wars*, Luke Skywalker is identified as a rebel. From the perspective of the Empire, Luke is an outlaw because he is a threat to the order of the Empire. In *The Lord of the Rings,* from the perspective of Lord Sauron, Frodo is an outlaw who must be stopped.

The early history of the United States is the story of outlaws who were determined to gain freedom from the British government. George Washington, Thomas Jefferson, Samuel Adams, Paul Revere, and Thomas

Paine—among others—were outlaws to the British Crown but have gone down in American history as heroes.

Consider the famous outlaw hero Robin Hood. Robin Hood has been the subject of numerous stories and legends, with widely different details. One version of the story is that the English king, Richard the Lionheart, went off on a crusade to rescue Jerusalem. During Richard's ten-year absence, his brother, the corrupt Prince John, abused the people by confiscating land and imposing severe taxes. In response to the corruption of John—or in some versions of the story, the Sheriff of Nottingham—Robin Hood gathered his band of Merry Men and began a campaign against the evil prince. Robin Hood is best known because he "stole from the rich to give to the poor."

Another Outlaw Hero

There is another outlaw hero who lived in a society that gathered the wealth of the land into the hands of a corrupt king. Most of the people in the land lived in fear of the king and the religious system. They were taxed heavily. Many lived in extreme poverty. To make matters even worse, the land was occupied by an invading imperial force. In the midst of the suffering of the people, various leaders arose to challenge the system. They rebelled against the evil of the society. For their efforts, they were executed by the government to put down attempted insurrection.

Who was this hero? His name was Jesus. Luke Skywalker, Robin Hood, and Jesus are all archetypal outlaws whose outlaw hero's journeys challenged the existing authority. The four gospel narratives in the New Testament are stories about an outlaw who challenged the authority system. If this seems too outrageous, ask yourself why Jesus was executed as a criminal. The power structure considered him dangerous and a threat to the social order.

Jesus the Outlaw

In the four gospel stories, Jesus is an outlaw hero who died an outlaw death. Although this is not the language of Christian tradition, stating it this way allows us to look at elements of the story that Christian tradition tends to overlook. In fact, recognizing that the four gospels are stories of Jesus as the outlaw hero make sense of the gospels stories ways that most of us have never understood.

Jesus has an outlaw perspective on money, power, and religion. Christian tradition often treats Jesus as a hero—the savior—without recognizing how much he was an outlaw hero against the dominant religious, political, and economic system.

From Outlaw to Savior

As the story of Jesus was told within Christian tradition, the meaning of the story changed. Jesus himself was redefined from outlaw hero to savior of souls. When you take the outlaw out of the hero, you take the outlaw character out of the stories about him.

When that happens, the outlaw money stories get turned on their heads. Then they become exactly what they were not intended to be. They become weapons against the weak. They turn outlaw condemnation of an economic system that impoverished people into a theological system teaching that Jesus wants people to be poor.

Injustice, Misery, and Evil

One of the enduring theological questions of any religious system is: Why is human life so full of misery and injustice? In Christian theology, the *theodicy question* asks: If God is all-good and God is all-powerful, why does evil exist in the world? Why do we suffer?

Every religion has its stories to answer such questions. Genesis has the story of Adam and Eve. This story explains how human beings were kicked out of paradise. The story also explains why we experience death, sickness, and suffering. Greek tradition has the *Hesiod* and the story about the creation of the first woman—Pandora—who brought evil to the paradisiacal world inhabited by men. (I won't even begin to discuss the inherent sexism of this story.) Babylonian tradition has the *Eluma Elish* that explains that human beings were created to serve the gods.

Whatever the tradition, stories give reasons for human misery and injustice. Stories also give reasons to hope that life on earth will be different. Someday it will be better.

Someday It Will Be Better

The idea of the kingdom of God, in all of its permutations, expresses this fundamental hope. Someday, God is going to make it better. Someday there will be justice instead of injustice. Someday, there will be health instead of sickness. Someday, there will be joy instead of mourning. Someday, there will be abundance instead of lack. Someday, the unjust will be punished and the innocent will be vindicated. Someday.

The worse life is on earth, the more people hope that God will make it better. Hebrew tradition has a category of writing called *apocalyptic*. Apocalyptic means *to reveal what is hidden.* Apocalyptic stories look forward to the time when God will bring justice and peace. The New Testament has an example of apocalyptic writing in the book of Revelation. Mark is the most apocalyptic of the gospels.

Jesus as the Christ

Both Matthew and Mark begin their narratives by identifying Jesus as *Christ* or *Messiah.* Luke goes through a lot of narrative before he reaches the point of identifying Jesus, but he too refers to Jesus as *Christ*.

Matthew, Mark, and Luke identify Jesus as the anointed one who will bring the kingdom of God on earth. *Christ* is the translation of the Hebrew word *messiah*. Messiah comes from the word that means *rubbed on*. During the rituals used to invest kings and priests into their offices, they were rubbed with oil—*anointed*—as a symbol of God's blessing. Most often, the term referred to the king.

Christian tradition is so used to separating religion from politics that it is not always evident that *Christ* as *Messiah* is a political designation. In Matthew, Mark, and Luke, Jesus is the anointed king who has come to announce that *someday* is now. The kingdom of God is at hand. Jesus has come to claim his authority to rule.

Chapter 9
Jesus Confronts the Threat

The instigating element of a hero's journey story is the *threat*. Something or someone threatens the wellbeing of the hero's world. Threats can come in all forms. The essential idea is that the hero is the one who must confront the threat at the location of its greatest power. This is why hero's journey stories are journeys. The hero must leave home to confront and defeat the threat. Only this heroic action can solve the problem that threatens the wellbeing of the hero's world.

The purpose of the hero's journey is to save the hero's world from the threat. All hero's journey stories are some form of *salvation* story and all heroes are *saviors*. Hero's journeys are not self-serving adventure stories, or stories of self-discovery, or stories about seeking rewards or treasure. Even though hero's journeys can be full of adventure and self-discovery and even treasure, the motive for the journey is salvation of others from the threat.

In addition, every hero's journey is both an outer journey and an inner journey.

The *outer journey* is the mission of the hero. The hero sets out on a journey to end the threat to the hero's world.

The *inner journey* concerns the inner struggles of the hero. The hero doesn't start out as a hero. Hero's journeys are about ordinary people who become heroes by the journey itself. Every hero must undergo some sort of death of the former self to become the savior.

The Threat in the Gospel Stories

The hero's journey is the story structure of the four New Testament Gospels. Since these gospel stories are textbook examples of hero's journey stories, the essential question is: Who or what needs to be saved from what threat? Are they really stories about how Jesus had to die on the cross to save you from your sinful nature?

If you ask this question as you read the four Christian gospels as hero's journey stories, you will see that the threat that motivates the hero's journey story about Jesus does not concern your sins. Rather, the threat concerns the abuses of power by the political, religious, and economic power located in Jerusalem.

The Hero's Mission

Each of the three synoptic gospels identifies the mission of the heroic journey:

Mission Statement in Mark

> Now after John was arrested, Jesus came into Galilee, preaching the gospel of God, and saying, "The time is fulfilled, and the kingdom of God is at hand; repent, and believe in the gospel" (Mark, 1:14, Revised Standard Version).

Mission Statement in Matthew

> From that time Jesus began to preach, saying, "Repent, for the kingdom of heaven is at hand" (Matthew 4: 17, Revised Standard Version).

Mission Statement in Luke

"The Spirit of the Lord is upon me, because he has anointed me to preach good news to the poor. He has sent me to proclaim release to the captives and recovering of sight to the blind, to set at liberty those who are oppressed, to proclaim the acceptable year of the Lord." ...And he began to say to them, "Today this scripture has been fulfilled in your hearing" (Luke 4:18-19, 21. Revised Standard Version).

These three statements are the programmatic statements of the hero's journey in each gospel. They capture the essence of the hero's journey for Jesus. At the same time, these statements demonstrate significant differences between the three gospel writers. Mark uses the phrase kingdom of God. Matthew follows Jewish tradition, which does not name God, but instead, uses a circumlocution. So Matthew refers to the kingdom of heaven, instead of the kingdom of God. Luke uses a reference from the Hebrew prophet Isaiah to make the concept of the kingdom of God clearer to a Gentile audience without using the term kingdom of God. Each makes clear that Jesus has accepted the hero's *call to adventure*.

Identifying the Threat

Each of these gospel narratives describes Jesus' hero's journey as a confrontation against those who hold power in his society. This challenge was political, religious, and economic. Power was concentrated in the composite of monarchy, temple, and upper class in an advanced agrarian economy. As if this was not enough, the whole region was under the heavy-handed domination of the Roman Empire. In short, his enemy was *Jerusalem*.

Jerusalem was the locus of power, where the monarchy, temple leaders, and Roman procurator were located. Used this way, *Jerusalem* is a figure of speech—a *metonymy*—in which Jerusalem stands for the entire power structure. In the same way, *Washington* is both the name of a place and a figure of speech for the entire complex of government located in Washington, D.C.

The Enemies of Jesus

The enemies of Jesus are the Scribes, Pharisees, Sadducees, Herodians, Chief Priests, Elders, and King Herod, among others. Jesus challenges the political, economic, religious system in very provocative ways. Everywhere he goes, he is the object of attention. Throughout the stories, Jesus encounters hostile official representatives who attempt to bait him into saying something incriminating.

A Political Demonstration

Meanwhile, Jesus provokes attention. He rides into Jerusalem on a donkey in front of people who know the scriptural tradition that the Messiah will enter Jerusalem on a donkey:

> Rejoice greatly, O daughter of Zion! Shout aloud, O daughter of Jerusalem! Lo, your king comes to you; triumphant and victorious is he, humble and riding on an ass, on a colt the foal of an ass (Zechariah 9:9).

Christians celebrate the event on Palm Sunday. What few Christians understand is how much this was a deliberate political demonstration and provocation. While the people cheered, *Jerusalem* regarded this entry as a flagrant claim to kingly power. In the phrase we hear too often, Jesus was "sending a message," using the shared cultural expectations of his society to make the statement: "I am the anointed one. I am the king."

The Church as Storyteller

The question I am raising here is: What kind of storytelling has Christian tradition done? Does the church tell stories about Jesus that grasp the essence of Jesus's outlaw hero's journey? Does the church teach that Jesus challenged a system that used power abusively? Or does the church tell stories about Jesus that are biblical urban legends, teaching people to obey those in power without challenging those who abuse their power in the name of God?

Part Four

Money Stories

of

Jesus

Chapter 10
God and Mammon

Treasures in Heaven
Matthew 6:19-24

Do not lay up for yourselves treasures on earth, where moth and rust consume and where thieves break in and steal, but lay up for yourselves treasures in heaven, where neither moth nor rust consumes and where thieves do not break in and steal. For where your treasure is, there will your heart be also. "The eye is the lamp of the body. So, if your eye is sound, your whole body will be full of light; but if your eye is not sound, your whole body will be full of darkness. If then the light in you is darkness, how great is the darkness! "No one can serve two masters; for either he will hate the one and love the other, or he will be devoted to the one and despise the other. You cannot serve God and mammon" (Matthew 6:19-24, Revised Standard Version).

"You cannot serve God and mammon." "Lay up treasures in heaven rather than treasures on earth." Taken together, these dual statements crystallize the problems of using Bible verses to create a doctrine of money.

They are also prime evidence for those who argue that "God does not want you to be rich." Taken as rules to live by, it's clear enough. This is exactly the problem with taking Bible verses out of context.

Biblical Urban Legends about God or Money

There has never been a single doctrine of money within the Christian church. The church has always been too theologically and culturally diverse to agree on anything as significant as money. However, the strongest tendency of the church has been to teach a doctrine of money that begins with these verses. The result is a "pie-in-the-sky" attitude toward life. Even if you are broke and hungry now, you will have everything you want in heaven—someday. Your goal is to focus on heaven because money is off-limits in this life. Taken as words without any larger context, these are very heavy words for people who are alive on Planet Earth.

When I was a child in Sunday school, my teachers used these verses to teach me that I had to choose between God and money. I couldn't have both.

Although I didn't realize it at the time, my teachers taught me a biblical urban legend. Words taken out of context turned into warnings: "Don't store up treasure on earth." "Don't serve mammon." In other words, money is bad stuff and heaven is at stake. We are left with a stark contrast. Live for heaven or live for now. Be rich now or have what you want later. As a doctrine of money, this doesn't help anyone learn to use money well and justly in this life.

The Words in Context

The only antidote to a biblical urban legend is to put the words into the whole story context of an agrarian society. In this context, Jesus is the outlaw hero. He sets out to challenge a social system in which wealth and power are concentrated in the hands of a few, leaving the rest of the society to suffer.

The Sermons "On the Mount" and "On the Plain"

The collection of material in Matthew 5-7 is traditionally called the *Sermon on the Mount*. The name comes from the introduction that "Jesus went up on the mountain." Luke has many of the same sayings in 6:17-49. The traditional name for the collection in Luke is the *Sermon on the Plain* since Luke says that Jesus "came down to them and stood on a level place."

Scholars claim that Matthew and Luke had a common set of source material called *Q*, (from the German word, *Quelle,* which means *source*). *Q* consisted of collected sayings of Jesus, probably in Aramaic. This creates an immediate problem for any attempt to put Bible verses back into their story contexts. There are no story contexts for the individual sayings. However, there is a story context for the whole collection.

The Gospel of Matthew and Torah

The Gospel of Matthew is laid out in a five part structure to match the five books of the Law—the Torah (Genesis, Exodus, Leviticus, Numbers, and Deuteronomy). In Matthew, the Sermon on the Mount is the first teaching collection. Jesus goes up on a mountain, sits down, and teaches. These details evoke comparison with Moses receiving the Ten Commandments on Mount Sinai. In Matthew, Jesus is the new Moses. Luke has much of the same material although it has been revised for Luke's Gentile Christian audience.

Even the detail that Jesus sits down to teach is an important clue that Matthew is addressing people steeped in Jewish tradition. Rabbis sit to teach. In contrast, Luke wrote his gospel for Gentile Christians who were used to having their teachers stand. In Luke, there is no mountain and Jesus stands to teach.

After making the point that all biblical sayings need to be read in context, I have extracted three short sections out of the Sermon on the Mount and the Sermon on the Plain to focus on specific words of Jesus. This chapter concerns *God and mammon*. Chapter 11 focuses on *bread and debts* in the Lord's Prayer. Chapter 12 focuses on the words from the Beatitudes, *blessed are the poor*. I have included both the Sermon on the Mount and the Sermon on the Plain in the Appendix. I encourage you to read through both of them in their entirety.

Teaching for Disciples

The most important point about context is that both the Sermon on the Mount and the Sermon on the Plain are addressed to disciples. Jesus is not addressing a hostile crowd or dealing with adversaries who are trying to trap him into saying something incriminating. He is teaching his followers about the good news of the kingdom of God.

For centuries, Christians have disagreed about the meaning of the teachings in the Sermon on the Mount and the Sermon on the Plain. Some claim that these teachings are impossible for human beings to follow in this age. They are simply descriptions of how disciples will live in a future time when God overthrows the rule of Satan and establishes the kingdom of God on earth in full power. Others claim that these are the rules for life here and now.

Mammon

Although the books of the New Testament were written in Greek, Jesus spoke Aramaic. *Mammon* is an Aramaic word. It originally referred to *prosperity* with no negative connotations. The meaning of the word itself evolved over time so that *mammon* became personified. *Mammon* is not just money. *Mammon* is wealth personified as a false god.

Jesus is making a contrast between trust in God and trust in personified material wealth.

This particular Bible verse raises specific translation issues. It is always a challenge to translate from one language to another in a way that accurately conveys the original meaning. In this instance, the translation challenge is whether to leave the Aramaic word *mammon* untranslated or to translate in a way that is meaningful for English-speaking readers. Earlier Biblical versions, such as the *King James Version* and the *Revised Standard Version*, left the Aramaic word untranslated. This means that English-speaking readers have no idea what it meant. More recent versions, such as the *New Revised Standard Version*, translate the word as *wealth*. This translation loses the broader meaning of the Aramaic word in which *mammon* is a godlike personification of wealth.

The Dualistic World View of Jesus

These words demonstrate the dualistic worldview of Jesus about his own society. He speaks in absolute terms with very little nuance. His statements have no middle ground. People are either disciples or adversaries. They are rich or poor. If they are rich, they are part of the oppressive ruling class. If they are poor, they are exploited by the powerful few. Jesus sees a world in conflict between two rulers—the rule of God and the rule of Satan. Here, Jesus contrasts God and the false god of wealth, Mammon.

English translations tend to soften the meaning of the statement about God and mammon by using the word *serve*. The more accurate translation is *to be a slave*. A slave owed the master exclusive and absolute obedience. This word slave makes the contrast even stronger. Jesus says that a disciple can only be a slave to one master, either God or mammon.

When my Sunday school teachers taught me that I had to choose between God and money, they were missing the forest for the trees. They taught me that only heaven matters, but life on earth is not important. To treat the sayings of Jesus as words denying the importance of life on earth is to deny the social justice emphasis of Jesus in his preaching the good news of the kingdom of God.

The Whole Story behind the Sermon on the Mount

The whole story context of these sayings is the background of Jesus' outlaw hero's journey. Jesus is confronting a social system in which most people suffered deprivation on earth. He clearly intends to address the injustices of his economic and religious system.

To take the words about injustice on earth and turn them into words about heaven misses this intention. He is proclaiming the Good News of the kingdom of God in an unjust agrarian society. To Jesus, the society is the problem. The kingdom of God is the solution. He is not claiming that life on earth doesn't matter. He is not claiming that the only solution to life on earth is getting into heaven. He is claiming that the kingdom of heaven needs to be established in full power on earth.

Chapter 11
Bread and Debts

The Lord's Prayer
Matthew 6:9-13

After this manner therefore pray ye: Our Father which art in heaven, Hallowed be thy name. Thy kingdom come. Thy will be done in earth, as [it is] in heaven. Give us this day our daily bread. And forgive us our debts, as we forgive our debtors. And lead us not into temptation, but deliver us from evil: For thine is the kingdom, and the power, and the glory, for ever. Amen. (Matthew 6:9-13, King James Version).

Pray then like this: Our Father who art in heaven, Hallowed be thy name. Thy kingdom come. Thy will be done, On earth as it is in heaven. Give us this day our daily bread; And forgive us our debts, As we also have forgiven our debtors; And lead us not into temptation, But deliver us from evil (Matthew 6:9-13, Revised Standard Version).

Pray then in this way: Our Father in heaven, hallowed be your name. Your kingdom come. Your will be done, on earth as it is in heaven. Give us this day our daily bread. And forgive us our debts, as we also have forgiven our debtors. And do not bring us to the time of trial, but rescue us from the evil one (Matthew 6:9-13, New Revised Standard Version).

The Lord's Prayer
Luke 11:1-4

And it came to pass, that, as he was praying in a certain place, when he ceased, one of his disciples said unto him, Lord, teach us to pray, as John also taught his disciples. And he said unto them, When ye pray, say, Our Father which art in heaven, Hallowed be thy name. Thy kingdom come. Thy will be done, as in heaven, so in earth. Give us day by day our daily bread. And forgive us our sins; for we also forgive every one that is indebted to us. And lead us not into temptation; but deliver us from evil" (Luke 11:1-4, King James Version).

He was praying in a certain place, and when he ceased, one of his disciples said to him, "Lord, teach us to pray, as John taught his disciples." And he said to them, "When you pray, say: "Father, hallowed be thy name. Thy kingdom come. Give us each day our daily bread; and forgive us our sins, for we ourselves forgive every one who is indebted to us; and lead us not into temptation" (Luke 11:1-4, Revised Standard Version).

He was praying in a certain place, and after he had finished, one of his disciples said to him, "Lord, teach us to pray, as John taught his disciples." He said to them, "When you pray, say: "Father, hallowed be your name. Your kingdom come. Give us each day our daily bread. And forgive our sins, for we ourselves forgive every one indebted to us. And do not bring us to the time of trial" (Luke 11:1-4, New Revised Standard Version).

One of the most familiar Bible passages is the *Lord's Prayer*. The prayer appears in both the Sermon on the Mount and the Sermon on the Plain. Although it is not immediately obvious to most people who pray this prayer, economic issues are at the heart of the prayer. I have included three translations of the prayer: the traditional *King James Version*; the *Revised Standard Version*; the *New Revised Standard Version*. Even though every Christian church uses the Lord's Prayer (following Matthew's version rather than Luke's), the exact wording varies.

Some churches retain the archaic English *thy* and *thine*. Protestant churches typically end the prayer with the phrase, "For thine is the kingdom and the power and the glory." Roman Catholic practice omits this phrase.

The most significant difference between various churches is that some churches use the language of *debts,* some use *trespasses,* and some use *sins.*

Who Were the Disciples?

This is the prayer for the disciples of Jesus. Who are the disciples? Although most people think of the disciples as the inner circle of twelve men surrounding Jesus, the word is used more than two hundred and fifty times in the Gospels and Acts and almost always refers to a larger group than the *Twelve*. The *disciples* are those who follow Jesus and believe in his teachings. They include both men and women from several social classes and ethnic backgrounds.

The Call to Discipleship

A disciple becomes a disciple through a direct invitation from Jesus. Following Jesus as a disciple means breaking all ties with the past, abandoning social ties, and renouncing all possessions. This is what Jesus asks the rich young man to do. Discipleship means living a socially uprooted life.

Disciples are artisans and craftsmen. They are tenant farmers. They are people who have been displaced from their land through the high rents and taxes imposed upon them. The sick and impoverished follow Jesus as his disciples. Many of the people surrounding Jesus are from the unclean and expendable classes.

One of the primary criticisms of Jesus by the Pharisees and scribes is that he associates with "sinners and tax collectors." He eats meals with people judged unclean by the religious law. He also eats meals with tax collectors who work for Rome to collect the taxes from the people. The tax collectors were universally hated.

The Twelve Disciples

The Twelve includes a diverse group, including Levi, one of the hated tax collectors, and Simon the Zealot, who was a political radical. It also includes the fishermen, Simon Peter and his brother, Andrew. Simon and Andrew are too poor to own a boat, so they cast nets into the water from the shore. James and John, the sons of Zebedee, are also fishermen but they have enough money to own a boat. They can fish directly from the water and afford to have hired help. The gospels give no information about the social status of the rest of the Twelve.

When Jesus teaches his followers to pray for daily bread and forgiveness of debts, the prayer is about more than spiritual sustenance and forgiveness of sins. He is first of all referring to real bread and real debts.

Forgiveness of Debts

The basic meaning of the Greek word *opheilemata* is *debts*. This financial meaning is consistent with the approach of Jesus to the social and ethical injustices of his society against the poor and dispossessed. In the prayer, he makes explicit the need for real bread and for payment of debt.

The prayer cannot be understood without also seeing it in terms of the kingdom of God. Before Jesus refers to bread and debts, he puts the prayer in the context of the kingdom of God. "Your kingdom come. Your will be done, on earth as it is in heaven."

Biblical Urban Legends about the Lord's Prayer

A prayer with the words: "Give us this day our daily bread and forgive us our debts, as we forgive our debtors" turns into a biblical urban legend when *bread* and *debt* become spiritual metaphors with no connection to real food and economic debt.

The Words in Context

For Jesus's audience, bread and debt were much more than metaphors. Hunger and debt were constant realities of life for an underfed, overtaxed population. Much of the misery of the peasants and beggars in Palestine resulted from debt. The peasants had to turn over much of what they grew to the king or other members of the urban elite class who claimed proprietary rights to whatever the peasants grew on the land. As a result, many of the peasant farmers were hopelessly in debt. Many of the beggars had been forced off their land by failure to pay their debts.

Jesus and Human Needs

Throughout the gospels, Jesus speaks about the real human needs of people in a society divided between the haves and the have-nots. He sees the vast gap between the rich and the poor and criticizes the rich for their exploitation and oppression of the poor. He also condemns a religious system that labels entire categories of people as *unclean*, a designation that excludes them from God's blessing.

He sees firsthand the extent of hunger, poverty, sickness, and suffering endured by most of the population. He sees how the rich landowners grow rich at the expense of the poor. He sees people who are homeless because they were driven off their land by high rents and taxes. He sees people living in poverty because the largest percentage of what they grow or make or catch is confiscated by taxes. He knows what it is like to live under Roman occupation where Roman soldiers could force people to do almost anything. He sees how the temple system collaborates with the Roman occupiers to bleed the people of their money and their power.

Forgiveness of Debts in the Hebrew Bible

One of the recurring themes of the Hebrew Bible is the periodic forgiveness of debts. Whether or not Israel ever put this system into actual practice, the scriptural tradition is very strong that the people of Israel would be released from their debts after specific periods of time. During the time of Jesus, Rabbi Hillel put into practice a system designed to regulate debts in accordance with Deuteronomy, which commands forgiveness of debts every seven years:

> Every seventh year you shall grant a remission of debts. And this is the manner of the remission: every creditor shall remit the claim that is held against a neighbor, not exacting it of a neighbor who is a member of the community, because the Lord's remission has been proclaimed. Of a foreigner you may exact it, but you must remit your claim on whatever any member of your community owes you. There will, however, be no one in need among you, because the LORD is sure to bless you in the land that the LORD your God is giving you as a possession to occupy (Deuteronomy 15:1-4, Revised Standard Version).

Debt and Sin

It is also true that the words of Jesus reflect Aramaic tradition that used *debt* as a metaphor for *sin*. Jesus spoke Aramaic. Aramaic writings show that the language of *debt* and *debtors* was used regularly for *sin* and *sinners*. Matthew's version of the Lord's Prayer preserves this Aramaic idiom. Here and elsewhere in Matthew, Jesus uses the double meaning of debts to refer to both real money debts and sins.

In Luke, the prayer uses the word *sin* rather than *debt*. This loses the financial reality behind the metaphor and obscures the underlying concern with real bread and real debts.

The coming of the kingdom of God means undoing the suffering and injustice of the current society. This also includes the forgiveness of real debts resulting from oppression, exploitation, and injustice.

Chapter 12
Blessed Are the Poor

The Beatitudes
Matthew 5:1-12

When Jesus saw the crowds, he went up the mountain; and after he sat down, his disciples came to him. Then he began to speak, and taught them, saying:

"Blessed are the poor in spirit, for theirs is the kingdom of heaven.

"Blessed are those who mourn, for they will be comforted.

"Blessed are the meek, for they will inherit the earth.

"Blessed are those who hunger and thirst for righteousness, for they will be filled.

"Blessed are the merciful, for they will receive mercy.

"Blessed are the pure in heart, for they will see God.

"Blessed are the peacemakers, for they will be called children of God.

"Blessed are those who are persecuted for righteousness' sake, for theirs is the kingdom of heaven.

"Blessed are you when people revile you and persecute you and utter all kinds of evil against you falsely on my account. Rejoice and be glad, for your reward is great in heaven, for in the same way they persecuted the prophets who were before you (Matthew 5:1-12, Revised Standard Version).

Beatitudes and Woes
Luke 6:17-26

And he came down with them and stood on a level place, with a great crowd of his disciples and a great multitude of people from all Judea and Jerusalem and the seacoast of Tyre and Sidon, who came to hear him and to be healed of their diseases; and those who were troubled with unclean spirits were cured. And all the crowd sought to touch him, for power came forth from him and healed them all. And he lifted up his eyes on his disciples, and said:

"Blessed are you poor, for yours is the kingdom of God.

"Blessed are you that hunger now, for you shall be satisfied.

"Blessed are you that weep now, for you shall laugh.

"Blessed are you when men hate you, and when they exclude you and revile you, and cast out your name as evil, on account of the Son of man! Rejoice in that day, and leap for joy, for behold, your reward is great in heaven; for so their fathers did to the prophets.

"But woe to you that are rich, for you have received your consolation. "Woe to you that are full now, for you shall hunger.

"Woe to you that laugh now, for you shall mourn and weep.

"Woe to you, when all men speak well of you, for so their fathers did to the false prophets" (Luke 6:17-26, Revised Standard Version).

Biblical Urban Legends about "Blessed Are the Poor"

For many Christians, "blessed are the poor" forms a counterpoint to "it is easier for a camel to go through the eye of a needle than for a rich man to enter the kingdom of God." These Bible verses create a double whammy. Not only is it bad to be rich, it's good to be poor. These words have produced their own biblical urban legends glorifying poverty in the name of Jesus. Once again, the only way to discern the real intention of the words is to put them into the dual contexts of gospel story and agrarian society.

The Words in Context

The statement "blessed are the poor" occurs in both Matthew and Luke. Matthew adds the words *in spirit*. Matthew begins the Sermon on the Mount with a set of nine statements traditionally called the *Beatitudes* from the Latin word meaning, *fortunate*, *happy*, or *blessed*. Luke has a list of four Beatitudes followed by four Woes.

To put the phrase *blessed are the poor* in context, we would need to look carefully at the whole set of Beatitudes in Matthew and the Beatitudes and Woes in Luke. Since we are looking at statements about money, we will look only at the first Beatitude, "Blessed are the poor" and the first Woe, "But woe to you that are rich, for you have received your consolation."

Blessed are the Beggars

The statement by Jesus—blessed are the poor—is a much more radical statement than most of us have ever realized. English Bibles translate the Greek word *ptochos* as *poor*. Greek has another word for *poor*, *penes*. *Penes* refers to people who have to work hard for a living, often struggling to make ends meet. In contrast, *ptochos* refers to someone who is utterly destitute and cut off from all family and social ties. In other words, a *ptochos* is a *beggar*.

In the advanced agrarian society in which Jesus lived, the *penes* were the peasant farmers and artisans struggling to earn a living in an unjust and oppressive system. The *ptochos* were the degraded and expendable people living at the very lowest levels of the society. The *ptochos* were unwanted, displaced, and rejected.

The kingdom of God Belongs to the Beggars

Leaving aside the difference between *poor in spirit* from Matthew and *poor* in Luke, both versions of the Beatitudes use the word *ptochos*. Both say that the kingdom of God belongs to the beggars, the destitute, and the expendables.

Once again, the key theme of everything Jesus says and does is the kingdom of God. Typically, Matthew appeals to Jewish Christian sensibilities by using kingdom of heaven rather than kingdom of God.

The Beatitudes in Matthew express Jesus' vision of the new reality for the beggars and outcasts. In Luke, the Beatitudes are followed by the Woes. Jesus contrasts the rich and the poor. The beggars and outcasts will receive God's blessing. In contrast, the rich will get nothing more. They have already gotten all they will get.

Confusion Description with Prescription

As soon as the phrase "blessed are the poor" is disconnected from the vision of the kingdom of God, it becomes a prime target for a makeover into a biblical urban legend. When I think back to my own Sunday school education, I am appalled by how often we were told that God wanted us to be poor. If being rich was going to keep us out of heaven, being poor was our best guarantee to get in.

The biggest mistake my Sunday School made is a common Christian misunderstanding of the Beatitudes. It confused *description* with *prescription*. We learned that we had to be poor in order to be blessed. We learned that God wanted us to be poor. We learned that Jesus was prescribing required behavior to get into heaven.

We didn't understand that Jesus was describing his vision of life under the kingdom of God. We didn't learn that Jesus was saying that even the poorest of the poor would receive God's blessing. That is the radical statement. Jesus was describing his vision of life on earth without poverty.

Overlooked Blessing

Besides not understanding the promise inherent in the kingdom of God, we also completely missed the importance of the word *blessed*. We memorized "blessed are the poor" and focused on being poor. We paid very little attention to the word *blessed*.

Blessing is one of my favorite biblical words. Over the years I taught in churches and in theological seminaries and as I had conversations with clergy friends, I asked a recurring question. I would ask these students and clergy friends to think about the story of creation in the first chapter of the Bible, Genesis 1. Then I asked: "After God created humankind in God's image, male and female, what was God's first action toward humankind?"

I asked lay people in churches. I asked students who were studying to become pastors, ministers, and priests. I asked people who were already pastors, ministers, and priests. Most said something about having dominion over the earth and being fruitful and multiplying. I heard the correct answer only once, from a student in one of my seminary classes. The correct answer is: *God blessed them*:

> So God created man in his own image, in the image
> of God he created him; male and female he created
> them. **And God blessed them**, [emphasis added] and

> God said to them, "Be fruitful and multiply, and fill
> the earth and subdue it; and have dominion over the
> fish of the sea and over the birds of the air and over
> every living thing that moves upon the earth." And
> God said, "Behold, I have given you every plant
> yielding seed which is upon the face of all the earth,
> and every tree with seed in its fruit; you shall have
> them for food. And to every beast of the earth, and
> to every bird of the air, and to everything that creeps
> on the earth, everything that has the breath of life, I
> have given every green plant for food." And it was
> so. And God saw everything that he had made, and
> behold, it was very good. And there was evening and
> there was morning, a sixth day (Genesis 1:27-30,
> Revised Standard Version).

The people I asked usually remembered the "be fruitful and multiply" language. They also usually remembered something about "dominion over the earth." But with one exception, no one remembered the language of blessing. I would then ask: "Why don't we know this?"

Two Conflicting Tendencies

Two conflicting tendencies exist in the Bible. The first tendency throughout the Bible moves toward expansion and abundance and inclusion. The creation story in Genesis 1 clearly demonstrates this tendency.

The second tendency moves toward contraction, lack, and exclusion. It is about rules, regulations, and restriction. It is based on a *pollution* system to define who is clean and who is unclean.

The current order of the biblical books is not chronological. The first chapter of Genesis is by no means the earliest material included in the Bible. The second creation story in Genesis, which begins in Chapter 2, is earlier material than the creation story in Chapter 1. Why did the editors who put the biblical writings together put the creation story in Genesis 1 first? I believe that they did so to provide a lens for reading everything that follows. Whatever else comes in the Bible, the Bible begins with God's intention to bless humanity.

The Meaning of Blessing

What does it mean *to bless* someone? Blessing expresses the desire for someone to experience all the abundance and goodness that life has to offer. Cursing is the opposite of blessing. A curse expresses the desire that someone experience all the bad that life has to offer.

Genesis 1 demonstrates the enormous power of words to create reality. In Genesis, bless is more than a statement of good intentions. Bless is an active verb. Genesis says that God created all living beings through God's words. With God's blessing, God created everything necessary for humankind to live lives of abundance.

Blessing and the Kingdom of God

Those words at the very beginning of Genesis also express the essence of the kingdom of God. In the kingdom of God, each human being is recognized as made in the image of God in relationship one to another. In the kingdom of God, human beings live lives of blessing and abundance. The vision of the kingdom of God is a society in which all people live their lives in the fullness of God's blessing.

Many of us never notice that God's primary action in Genesis 1 is to bless with abundance because we have been so conditioned toward the tendency toward limitation and restriction. Many religious groups focus on what we should do and shouldn't do. They look at ways to separate themselves from others. They teach exclusion, restriction, and limitation. They teach fear. Their Bible is a *Constraining Bible* rather than a *Liberating Bible*.

The Pharisees

The Pharisees are adversaries that Jesus meets again and again in the gospel stories. We will encounter them again in other stories about Jesus and his statements about money. The root meaning of the word Pharisee is *separation*. The Pharisees were devout laymen who were determined to follow the strictest rules of their religion. They were quick to judge when someone failed to follow the rules. They are representative of the tendency toward restrictions, limitations, and separation.

Abundance or Lack?

When it comes to the topic of money, the same two tendencies operate. One constricts and one expands. One constrains and one liberates. The constraining tendency teaches lack and doing without as God's will. Many of us grew up with religious training that taught us restrictions and rules and exclusions. Instead of God's promise of abundance, we learned that God wants us to live lives of lack and limitation. We learned that poverty is the price of blessing.

It's both astonishing and disturbing that so many Christians can memorize something called the Beatitudes and think that Jesus intends to preach poverty without understanding that the intention of the sayings is to bless those who are now the poorest of the poor. All but one of the people I asked about Genesis 1 didn't even remember the words: *God blessed them.*

This type of teaching is the reason that the Prosperity Camp exists. Prosperity teachers are reacting against the type of Christian teaching that makes poverty a condition of God's blessing.

Jesus' Radical Claim

In the context of the story of Jesus' hero's journey, within the social context of the agrarian society, Jesus makes the radical claim that the kingdom of God will bless the ones the existing religious system refuses to bless.

The critical point is that Jesus is not blessing poverty. He is blessing the poorest of the poor. In the kingdom of God, even the beggars are blessed.

Chapter 13
Taxes to Caesar

Render to Caesar
Matthew 22:15-22

Then the Pharisees went and took counsel how to entangle him in his talk. And they sent their disciples to him, along with the Herodians, saying, "Teacher, we know that you are true, and teach the way of God truthfully, and care for no man; for you do not regard the position of men. Tell us, then, what you think. Is it lawful to pay taxes to Caesar, or not?" But Jesus, aware of their malice, said, "Why put me to the test, you hypocrites? Show me the money for the tax." And they brought him a coin. And Jesus said to them, "Whose likeness and inscription is this?" They said, "Caesar's." Then he said to them, "Render therefore to Caesar the things that are Caesar's, and to God the things that are God's." When they heard it, they marveled; and they left him and went away (Matthew 22:15-22, Revised Standard Version).

Render to Caesar
Mark 12:13-17

And they sent to him some of the Pharisees and some of the Herodians, to entrap him in his talk. And they came and said to him, "Teacher, we know that you are true, and care for no man; for you do not regard the position of men, but truly teach the way of God. Is it lawful to pay taxes to Caesar, or not?

Should we pay them, or should we not?" But knowing their hypocrisy, he said to them, "Why put me to the test? Bring me a coin, and let me look at it." And they brought one. And he said to them, "Whose likeness and inscription is this?" They said to him, "Caesar's." Jesus said to them, "Render to Caesar the things that are Caesar's, and to God the things that are God's." And they were amazed at him (Mark 12:13-17, Revised Standard Version).

Render to Caesar
Luke 20:19-26

The scribes and the chief priests tried to lay hands on him at that very hour, but they feared the people; for they perceived that he had told this parable against them. So they watched him, and sent spies, who pretended to be sincere, that they might take hold of what he said, so as to deliver him up to the authority and jurisdiction of the governor. They asked him, "Teacher, we know that you speak and teach rightly, and show no partiality, but truly teach the way of God. Is it lawful for us to give tribute to Caesar, or not?" But he perceived their craftiness, and said to them, "Show me a coin. Whose likeness and inscription has it?" They said, "Caesar's." He said to them, "Then render to Caesar the things that are Caesar's, and to God the things that are God's." And they were not able in the presence of the people to catch him by what he said; but marveling at his answer they were silent (Luke 20:19-26, Revised Standard Version).

If anyone has any idea that money is simply a matter of personal morality, this episode brings to the surface the relationship between religion and government. This is a story about taxation. But it is about more than taxation. It involves questions of authority on earth. Do believers obey God or the government? Interpretation of this particular episode goes far beyond money. The Bible verse, "Then render to Caesar the things that are Caesar's, and to God the things that are God's," is responsible for shameful moments in church history when Christian churches kept silent while governments perpetrated atrocities.

Jesus, the Watched Man

But I am getting ahead of the story. This episode shows that Jesus is a watched man. Throughout the gospel narratives, Jesus has several groups of people from the ruling class following him. They are listening and looking for anything they can use to turn him over to the Roman authorities.

Significant names appear in this episode: Caesar; the Pharisees; the Herodians; the Scribes; and the Chief Priests. These names represent three overlapping and intersecting political power structures: the Roman Empire; the Jewish monarchy; and the Jerusalem temple.

Caesar Augustus

Caesar was the Roman emperor, Caesar Augustus. A significant reality of the life and words of Jesus as recorded in the four gospels is that Palestine (Judea to the Jews) was occupied by the troops of the Roman Empire.

Pontius Pilate

Roman Palestine was administered by a Roman official called the procurator. It's worth pondering the meaning of the word *procure* in English.

According to Merriam-Webster, *procure* means "to get possession of: obtain by particular care and effort." (The second meaning is "to get and make available for promiscuous sexual intercourse.")

In other words, the primary role of procurators of occupied territories was to extract as much wealth as possible from the region under their control for the empire.

At the same time, procurators extracted as much wealth as possible for themselves. It was the ancient Roman version of a retirement plan. After service in some remote region of the empire, a procurator could return to Rome and live in luxury with the money he had extorted from the occupied region.

Pontius Pilate was the procurator of Judea at the time. Although Lenten readings in churches sometimes convey the impression that Pontius Pilate was reluctant to send Jesus to his death, historical sources describe Pontius Pilate as a particularly cruel and greedy administrator who flagrantly abused his power. Pontius Pilate was also known to deliberately provoke Jewish piety by minting coins with images designed to offend Jews.

The Pharisees

The Pharisees were laymen. However, they followed the strict rules for priests in their own personal piety. They also demanded that others do the same. The Pharisees were ardent defenders of the status quo. They collaborated with the temple leadership, the Jewish monarchy, and the Roman rulers. Throughout the gospels, the Pharisees appear several times as spies who are looking for ways to trap Jesus into doing or saying something contrary to religious law and governmental law.

The Herodians

The Herodians were supporters of the Jewish King Herod Antipas. Herod was a typical king in an agrarian society. He claimed ownership over all the land he ruled. He used his power to extract wealth from the population. Since Herod ruled at the will of Rome, he collaborated with Roman imperial power to keep his throne. The Herodians also appear in the gospel narratives as men who are spying on Jesus to find evidence that he was undermining the political power of the king.

The Scribes

The scribes were the legal scholars. In a culture in which almost no one could read or write, the scribes were literate. They were the experts in both the oral and written law— the Torah. They were the lawyers and judges who ruled on questions of the ritual law. In several episodes of the gospels, they appear with the Pharisees and share the same motive. They are trying to find evidence to prove that Jesus is violating Torah.

The Chief Priests

The chief priests controlled the Jerusalem temple. After Pontius Pilate, who was the Roman procurator, the most powerful man in Roman-occupied Palestine was the high priest, identified in the gospels as Caiaphas. Caiaphas was a willing collaborator with Rome.

The chief priests were the board of directors of the temple. They set the policies of the temple and supervised the temple's two basic functions. A temple was the center of worship and it collected taxes.

A significant part of worship was the ritual sacrifice of animals on the central altar. This meant that worshippers either brought their own animals and birds or they bought them at the temple. The chief priests allowed the sale of animals used in the daily sacrifices through a concession system.

The chief priests also collected the taxes and tithes imposed upon the people. They distributed the money to the monarchy, the priesthood, and the Roman occupiers.

Both of these factors are significant in the story of Jesus driving out the money changers.

Taxes to the Emperor

In this episode, Matthew and Mark say that the Pharisees and Herodians are trying to trap Jesus. Luke has the scribes and chief priests sending spies to do the same thing. Luke states explicitly that the motive is to find a way to turn Jesus over to the Roman governor Pontius Pilate. The focus of the trap concerns paying taxes to the emperor.

From the time of the Roman conquest of Palestine in 6 C.E., Rome demanded and collected direct taxes from the people. Government officials collected land taxes, a *poll* on each person, taxes on personal property, and taxes on the transport of goods. The question to Jesus concerns the payment of the poll tax.

The motive behind asking the question is easy to understand. Most of us don't much like paying taxes to our own government. We would be even less eager to pay taxes to an occupying force. In fact, the precipitating grievance that led to the American Revolution was taxation without representation. The colonists declared independence to avoid paying taxes to the British crown.

Resistance to the Roman Occupation

The occupied people of Palestine hated paying taxes to their Roman occupiers. The people considered themselves oppressed people under military occupation. From time to time, various messianic and revolutionary groups formed in opposition to the Roman occupiers and the Jewish collaborators. Occasionally, an open rebellion broke out and was quickly crushed by the ruling powers.

These revolutionary groups regarded any collaboration with the hated Roman occupiers as treason to God. Refusal to pay the Roman taxes was an act of defiance against the oppressors and an act of allegiance to God.

Looking for Evidence

When these various collaborators with Rome ask Jesus about paying the temple tax, they are looking for evidence that he is one of the revolutionaries so they can hand him over to the authority of Pontius Pilate. Luke makes this clear:

> So they watched him, and sent spies, who pretended to be sincere, that they might take hold of what he said, so as to deliver him up to the authority and jurisdiction of the governor   (Luke 20:20, Revised Standard Version).

In all three versions of the story, Jesus asks to see the coin used for the poll tax. The particular coin is an important part of the story.

The Roman Denarius

During the time of Jesus, several types of coins were commonly used. The Romans minted their own silver coins in Rome and other imperial mints. One of these Roman coins was the *denarius*. The denarius the accepted daily wage for a common laborer. The Roman coins had an image of the emperor on the front side of the coin. The coin handed to Jesus was probably the silver denarius bearing the image of Caesar Augustus.

By asking whose image and inscription are on the coin, Jesus successfully avoids the trap. When his questioners identify Caesar, Jesus says, "Render to Caesar what belongs to Caesar." In other words, he says, "pay the tax." He is not openly advocating civil disobedience against the

Roman authorities on the matter of taxation—a stance which would have given the Romans immediate cause to arrest him.

Luther's Theology of the Two Kingdoms

Although Jesus avoided the trap in the story, Christian history has used these words to draw a line between church and state. The most notable is Martin Luther's theology of the two kingdoms. The church would administer the spiritual realm while worldly governments would rule the secular realm. Although Luther's theology was more complicated than this, his two kingdoms theology led to the idea that believers owed allegiance and obedience to the worldly ruler on matters of the state.

Luther and the Peasants War

In a situation with many similarities to the Jewish Revolt against Rome, which began in 66 A.D., the German peasants rebelled against their agrarian overlords in the Peasants' War, 1524–26. They thought that Luther's stance supported their cause. However, in one of the most controversial decisions of his life, Luther invoked the two kingdoms theology to condemn the revolt, based on the idea that the political leadership was ordained by God to rule on earth. The revolt failed and reinforced the long-standing belief that human beings owe allegiance on earth to their human rulers.

Separation of Church and State in Nazi Germany

During the Nazi era, most Christian churches in Germany maintained this separation between church and state. The church ruled on spiritual matters. The government ruled on secular matters. Only a few churches, known as the Confessing Church, defied Hitler's claim to power with predictable results. Many died for opposing the power of the government.

Although this brief historical foray might seem off-track from our consideration of the stories about money, it demonstrates at least two critical points. The first is that nothing good happens when people build any kind of theology on single Bible verses.

The Words in Context

The second is to insist once again that the Bible verses must be put into the context of the gospel story in the context of the agrarian society. In the gospel stories, Jesus is on a campaign to challenge the abuse of power by the monarchy, the landholders, the temple leadership, and the occupying empire.

Once again, we come back to the same point. The kingdom of heaven is not equivalent to heaven. Jesus intends to make life better on this earth. The words of Jesus get him off the hook in the story. However, the legacy of these words leads to complex and difficult questions about the power of governments and the allegiance of believers.

Chapter 14
The Money Changers

Jesus and the Money Changers
Mark 11:15-18

And they came to Jerusalem. And he entered the temple and began to drive out those who sold and those who bought in the temple, and he overturned the tables of the money-changers and the seats of those who sold pigeons; and he would not allow any one to carry anything through the temple. And he taught, and said to them, "Is it not written, My house shall be called a house of prayer for all the nations'? But you have made it a den of robbers." And the chief priests and the scribes heard it and sought a way to destroy him; for they feared him, because all the multitude was astonished at his teaching (Mark 11:15-18, Revised Standard Version).

Jesus and the Money Changers
Matthew 21:12-16

And Jesus entered the temple of God and drove out all who sold and bought in the temple, and he overturned the tables of the money-changers and the seats of those who sold pigeons. He said to them, "It is written, My house shall be called a house of prayer'; but you make it a den of robbers" (Matthew 21:12-16, Revised Standard Version).

Jesus and the Money Changers
Luke 19:45-48

And he entered the temple and began to drive out those who sold, saying to them, "It is written, My house shall be a house of prayer'; but you have made it a den of robbers." And he was teaching daily in the temple. The chief priests and the scribes and the principal men of the people sought to destroy him; but they did not find anything they could do, for all the people hung upon his words (Luke 19:45-48, Revised Standard Version).

Jesus and the Money Changers
John 2:14-17

In the temple he found those who were selling oxen and sheep and pigeons, and the money-changers at their business. And making a whip of cords, he drove them all, with the sheep and oxen, out of the temple; and he poured out the coins of the money-changers and overturned their tables. And he told those who sold the pigeons, "Take these things away; you shall not make my Father's house a house of trade." His disciples remembered that it was written, "Zeal for thy house will consume me" (John 2:14-17, Revised Standard Version).

Since the story about Jesus driving the money changers out of the temple occurs in all four gospels, I also include the quotation from John. This is obviously an important story in the traditions about Jesus for all four gospels to include it.

Biblical Urban Legends about the Money Changers

This episode leads to at least two different biblical urban legends. The first concerns the money changers in the temple. According to this interpretation, the idea of having money changers in the temple was so reprehensible that Jesus had to drive them out. This is consistent with the statement of Jesus that you cannot serve God and mammon. You cannot mix God and money.

Anger

The second biblical urban legend concerns anger. This story says that Jesus gets angry. One version of the urban legend is that Jesus is justified in his anger because money simply doesn't belong in the temple. Another version of the biblical urban legend concerns anger itself along the lines of: "Jesus said in the Sermon on the Mount that we are supposed to turn the other cheek (Matthew 5:39) and not get angry." Yet here, Jesus goes on a rampage through the temple.

From my observation of discussions on this story, Jesus comes out ahead in both cases. If the emphasis is on money, the consensus is that Jesus was justifiably angry about merchants doing business in the temple. If the emphasis is on anger, Jesus still comes out ahead. Since Jesus was righteous in everything he did, his anger was also righteous. The implied implication of this tack is that the rest of us are not so righteous and so our anger is rarely justified.

What's Missing?

What is most revealing is that neither of these biblical urban legends attempts to explain who the money changers were and what they were doing in the temple. They also don't explain the functions of a temple.

With no understanding of the role of the temple and no understanding of the role of money changers in the temple, the episode of Jesus driving out the money changers becomes simply a cautionary tale about the evils of mixing religion and money or a story about justified anger in a righteous cause.

The Temple

Before identifying the money changers, we need to consider the temple itself. Throughout the Ancient Near East, a temple was regarded as the symbolic dwelling place of a god. The temple was the house of the god who ruled the land. The essential fact about a temple that I never learned in Sunday School is that a temple is very different from a church. *Church (ecclesia)* means *gathered community*. A church building is the place where the church gathers. The building is not the church. The people are the church.

Holy Space

A critical factor about the temple was the importance of holy space. The temple comprised several zones of sacred space. [If you are interested in more detail about temples and holy space, see my doctoral dissertation, *The Vision of Transformation.*]

Access to the Temple Building

The lay people never went into the temple building. Only priests could enter the temple building itself. They entered the building only in highly controlled situations. Since the priests were the house-servants of the god, the priests could go inside the building to tend to the needs of the god dwelling inside. In the Jerusalem temple, the symbolic dwelling place of God was the section of the temple building called the *Holy of Holies*. Only the high priest could enter this area and only once a year, on the day of purification—*Yom Kippur*.

Access to the Altar and Courtyards

Worship consisted of offering prayers and sacrifices. Only the priests could approach the altar in the inner court. No lay person could approach the altar. A lay person would pay to have the offering presented by the priests.

The temple was built with various open courtyards, at different elevations. It had a courtyard for the adult Jewish males who were not priests, a courtyard for women, and a courtyard for Gentiles farthest away from the altar. In other words, controlling who was allowed access to various spaces was vitally important.

The Temples Were Also Banks

In addition to being a location for worship, temples were the banks of the ancient world. Temples stored valuables. They made loans. They collected taxes. They were also places to change currencies.

Currencies

Ancient Palestine had no standard currency. Jerusalem was a cosmopolitan city. The Herodian kings printed their own currency, usually in bronze. The Roman procurators minted their own coins, usually in silver. Roman soldiers brought various Roman coins with them that had been minted in Rome. Neighboring city-states minted their own currencies in copper, bronze, and silver. This means that people doing any sort of commerce in Palestine had access to and used a multitude of currencies. All of these coins had different sizes and weights.

The Denarius

What is even more significant is that certain coins had become the standard for particular functions. The typical day's wage was a denarius, which was a Roman silver coin, with the image of Caesar on it. The denarius was also the coin used for the poll tax—the subject of the comment about rendering to Caesar what belonged to Caesar.

The Temple Tax

In addition to the heavy taxes and rents demanded by the ruling class and the taxes paid to the Romans, every Jewish male over the age of twenty, whether living in Palestine or elsewhere, was required to pay an annual temple tax. During the lifetime of Jesus, the tax was one-half shekel, to be paid in the period before Passover.

My sources disagree on the coin required for the temple tax. Some claim that it was the Roman silver denarius with the image of Caesar. Others claim that it was the silver shekel minted in Tyre. That coin bore the image of the pagan god Baal.

Whether the required coin for the temple tax was the Roman denarius with the image of Caesar or the Tyrian shekel with the image of Baal, the administration of the temple required payment of the temple tax with a coin bearing an image of an emperor or a pagan god. This is especially incongruous considering that Hebrew religion always prohibited the use of idols and images of God.

Fortunately for us, we don't need to identify the specific coins used to pay the temple tax. The important point is that the people of Roman Palestine used multiple currencies and had to use different currencies for different purposes.

The Essential Role of the Money Changers

With all of these currencies in common use, each made of different metals and weights, money changers played an essential role. They did many of the functions of modern bankers, whether in the outlying regions or at the temple itself. They changed currencies and made change. Not surprisingly, they charged fees for their services.

The Merchants

In addition to the money changers, the episode refers to merchants who sold birds and animals for the sacrifices. These merchants were also performing an essential service by providing the birds and animals necessary for worshippers to offer required sacrifices. Without these merchants, people who lived in cities had no way to provide the creatures used in sacrifices, and people who lived at a distance from Jerusalem would have to transport their creatures to the temple.

Both the money changers and the merchants of birds and livestock operated under the authority of the temple administration to allow the people to participate in the required rituals and payments to the temple.

Why Did Jesus Take Offense?

The significant question is: Why did Jesus take such offense at the presence of the money changers and the merchants in the temple?

Jesus apparently didn't object to paying the required temple tax. Matthew records a rather strange story about Jesus telling Peter to pay the temple tax for both of them with the coin retrieved from the mouth of a fish:

> When they came to Capernaum, the collectors of the half-shekel tax went up to Peter and said, "Does not your teacher pay the tax?" He said, "Yes." And when he came home, Jesus spoke to him first, saying, "What do you think, Simon? From whom do kings of the earth take toll or tribute? From their sons or from others?" And when he said, "From others," Jesus said to him, "Then the sons are free. However,

not to give offense to them, go to the sea and cast a
hook, and take the first fish that comes up, and when
you open its mouth you will find a shekel; take that
and give it to them for me and for yourself"
(Matthew 17:24-27, Revised Standard Version).

Speculations

Since the four passages about the money changers don't
really explain exactly what set Jesus off on his rampage,
people are left to speculate.

One speculation is that the money changers were
charging excessive fees for exchanging currencies.

Another speculation concerns location. Only Mark
includes the detail that Jesus "would not allow any one to
carry anything through the temple." Perhaps the money
changers and animal and bird sellers were set up in an
area that Jesus thought was violating holy space.

Perhaps there was loud haggling over rates and the
sounds of animal and birds, interfering with prayer and
worship.

The Outlaw Hero Explanation

From the perspective of the hero's journey, the most likely
reason is that Jesus is fulfilling his call to adventure as the
outlaw hero. He confronts the system at its source. Mark,
Matthew, and Luke include a quotation from the prophet
Jeremiah, which identifies the temple as a "den of robbers":

> The word that came to Jeremiah from the LORD:
> "Stand in the gate of the LORD's house, and proclaim
> there this word, and say, Hear the word of the LORD,
> all you men of Judah who enter these gates to
> worship the LORD. Thus says the LORD of hosts, the
> God of Israel, Amend your ways and your doings, and
> I will let you dwell in this place. Do not trust in these

deceptive words: This is the temple of the LORD, the temple of the LORD, the temple of the LORD.' "For if you truly amend your ways and your doings, if you truly execute justice one with another, if you do not oppress the alien, the fatherless or the widow, or shed innocent blood in this place, and if you do not go after other gods to your own hurt, then I will let you dwell in this place, in the land that I gave of old to your fathers for ever." Behold, you trust in deceptive words to no avail. Will you steal, murder, commit adultery, swear falsely, burn incense to Ba'al, and go after other gods that you have not known, and then come and stand before me in this house, which is called by my name, and say, We are delivered!' -- only to go on doing all these abominations? Has this house, which is called by my name, become a den of robbers in your eyes? Behold, I myself have seen it, says the LORD. (Jeremiah 7:1-11, Revised Standard Version).

The episode in the temple is part of Jesus' self-conscious challenge to business as usual. The outlaw hero Jesus stages a dramatic performance to challenge the political and religious structure of his time. It serves the same purpose as any kind of protest demonstration in our own era. When people march on Washington, whether for or against any type of government policy, they are demonstrating to make a point. Jesus is also demonstrating to make a point in the temple.

The stories also demonstrate that Jesus was increasingly popular with the people and increasingly unpopular with the leadership. In other words, he continued to make both disciples and enemies.

The Relationship between Church and State

The episode with the temple tax raises questions about the relationship between church and state. The temple was part of the state and served as the money collector for the government. This story about the money changers raises additional questions that I will raise but not attempt to discuss.

In addition, this story brings to the surface all kinds of questions about churches and money in our own political and religious system. Churches in the United States are tax-free entities as long as they remain politically neutral.

It also raises questions about running churches as businesses. When do churches cross the line from non-profit to for-profit entities?

Are churches supposed to be poor? Or are churches supposed to be rich?

When does the church become part of the system, adopting the material values of the society?

When does it see itself as a prophetic voice against the system, living out of a vision of the kingdom of God?

These are all hermeneutical questions rather than exegetical ones and so I leave them as open questions for you to ponder.

Chapter 15
Honor Your Father
And Your Mother

Honor Your Father and Your Mother
Mark 7:1-13

Now when the Pharisees gathered together to him, with some of the scribes, who had come from Jerusalem, they saw that some of his disciples ate with hands defiled, that is, unwashed. (For the Pharisees, and all the Jews, do not eat unless they wash their hands, observing the tradition of the elders; and when they come from the market place, they do not eat unless they purify themselves; and there are many other traditions which they observe, the washing of cups and pots and vessels of bronze.) And the Pharisees and the scribes asked him, "Why do your disciples not live according to the tradition of the elders, but eat with hands defiled?" And he said to them, "Well did Isaiah prophesy of you hypocrites, as it is written, This people honors me with their lips, but their heart is far from me; in vain do they worship me, teaching as doctrines the precepts of men.' You leave the commandment of God, and hold fast the tradition of men." And he said to them, "You have a fine way of rejecting the commandment of God, in order to keep your tradition! For Moses said, Honor your father and your mother'; and, He who speaks evil of father or mother, let him surely die'; but you say, If a man tells his father or his mother,

What you would have gained from me is Corban'
(that is, given to God) -- then you no longer permit
him to do anything for his father or mother, thus
making void the word of God through your tradition
which you hand on. And many such things you do"
(Mark 7:1-13, Revised Standard Version).

Honor Your Father and Your Mother
Matthew 15: 1-6

Then Pharisees and scribes came to Jesus from
Jerusalem and said, "Why do your disciples
transgress the tradition of the elders? For they do
not wash their hands when they eat." He answered
them, "And why do you transgress the
commandment of God for the sake of your tradition?
For God commanded, Honor your father and your
mother,' and, He who speaks evil of father or
mother, let him surely die.' But you say, If any one
tells his father or his mother, What you would have
gained from me is given to God, he need not honor
his father.' So, for the sake of your tradition, you
have made void the word of God (Matthew 15: 1-6,
Revised Standard Version).

Religious Law and the Vulnerable

At first glance, this statement might seem to be out of place
as a money story. The command to honor father and mother
is one of the Ten Commandments from Exodus 20 and
Deuteronomy 5. However, it belongs among the money
sayings of Jesus because it concerns financial responsibility
to elderly parents. This saying and the saying about the
poor widow in the next chapter involve use of the religious
law to impoverish the vulnerable.

Of all of the enemies Jesus encounters, the Pharisees
and scribes are ones most likely to start a challenge by

citing scripture. These enemies ask questions designed to trap Jesus into some statement contrary to the Torah. In this story, they want to know why he and his disciples are not following the required ritual hand washing before meals. Jesus turns the encounter on its head and asks: "Why do you not follow the command to honor your father and your mother?"

Before considering why this commandment belongs among the money statements, we need to consider two factors.

The Patriarchal Family

First, the basic unit of the society in which Jesus lived was the patriarchal family. In ancient Israel, this family structure was called the *house of the father* (*beth ab*). The eldest male ruled as the head of the household. Several generations of family members lived on the family land under the authority of the father. Everyone in the household was required to submit to the authority of the adult male as the head of the family.

When the father died, the authority of the family unit passed to the oldest son. This meant that younger brothers and their families also lived under the authority of the oldest son. Sometimes, the father would pass on his authority before he died, leaving the oldest son to rule as the head of the household while his father was still alive.

Ten Commandments in Exodus
Exodus 20:1-17

And God spoke all these words, saying, "I am the LORD your God, who brought you out of the land of Egypt, out of the house of bondage. "You shall have no other gods before me. "You shall not make for yourself a graven image, or any likeness of anything that is in heaven above, or that is in the earth beneath, or that is in the water under the earth; you shall not bow down to them or serve them; for I the LORD your God am a jealous God, visiting the iniquity of the fathers upon the children to the third and the fourth generation of those who hate me, but showing steadfast love to thousands of those who love me and keep my commandments. "You shall not take the name of the LORD your God in vain; for the LORD will not hold him guiltless who takes his name in vain. "Remember the sabbath day, to keep it holy. Six days you shall labor, and do all your work; but the seventh day is a sabbath to the LORD your God; in it you shall not do any work, you, or your son, or your daughter, your manservant, or your maidservant, or your cattle, or the sojourner who is within your gates; for in six days the LORD made heaven and earth, the sea, and all that is in them, and rested the seventh day; therefore the LORD blessed the sabbath day and hallowed it. "Honor your father and your mother, that your days may be long in the land which the LORD your God gives you. "You shall not kill. "You shall not commit adultery. "You shall not steal. "You shall not bear false witness against your neighbor." You shall not covet your neighbor's house; you shall not covet your neighbor's wife, or his manservant, or his maidservant, or his ox, or his ass, or anything that is your neighbor's" (Exodus 20:1 17, Revised Standard Version).

Ten Commandments in Deuteronomy
Deuteronomy 5:6-21

"I am the LORD your God, who brought you out of the land of Egypt, out of the house of bondage." You shall have no other gods before me. "You shall not make for yourself a graven image, or any likeness of anything that is in heaven above, or that is on the earth beneath, or that is in the water under the earth; you shall not bow down to them or serve them; for I the LORD your God am a jealous God, visiting the iniquity of the fathers upon the children to the third and fourth generation of those who hate me, but showing steadfast love to thousands of those who love me and keep my commandments. "You shall not take the name of the LORD your God in vain: for the LORD will not hold him guiltless who takes his name in vain. "Observe the sabbath day, to keep it holy, as the LORD your God commanded you. Six days you shall labor, and do all your work; but the seventh day is a sabbath to the LORD your God; in it you shall not do any work, you, or your son, or your daughter, or your manservant, or your maidservant, or your ox, or your ass, or any of your cattle, or the sojourner who is within your gates, that your manservant and your maidservant may rest as well as you. You shall remember that you were a servant in the land of Egypt, and the LORD your God brought you out thence with a mighty hand and an outstretched arm; therefore the LORD your God commanded you to keep the sabbath day. "Honor your father and your mother, as the LORD your God commanded you; that your days may be prolonged, and that it may go well with you, in the land which the LORD your God gives you. "You shall not kill. "Neither shall you commit adultery." Neither shall you steal. "Neither shall you bear false witness against your neighbor." Neither shall you covet your neighbor's wife; and you shall not desire your neighbor's house, his field, or his manservant, or his maidservant, his ox, or his ass, or anything that is your neighbor's' (Deuteronomy 5: 6-21, Revised Standard Version).

The Ten Commandments
and the Head of the Household

In Exodus and Deuteronomy, these words are addressed to the male head of the multigenerational family living on the family land in an agrarian society. The reference to the third and fourth generation refers to several generations of the family living on the same plot of land at the same time. It is not a reference to the effect on future generations. It also explains why the prohibition is against coveting the neighbor's wife, with no mention of coveting the neighbor's husband.

The command to honor father and mother is clearly addressed to the adult head of the household about his responsibility to his aged parents. If a son becomes the head of the household before his parents die, he is responsible for their care.

The Biblical Urban Legend about
"Honor Your Father and Your Mother"

Despite this original context, the command to "honor your father and your mother" has become a biblical urban legend about the obedience of children to parental authority. The original Hebraic meaning got lost as the church moved into the Gentile world.

Even though the word *honor* is not equivalent to the word *obedience,* and even though the words originally referred to the adult head of the household, countless generations of Christian children have been taught that the words apply to them. The *Family Circus* ran a cartoon expressing this belief. It shows Dolly pointing to the Bible and telling her younger brother: "It's right here in the Bible. You have to do 'zactly what thy mommy and thy daddy tell you to do."

The original commandment to the male head of the household commanding him to take care of his elderly parents turned into a command that children must obey their parents.

Corban

The word *Corban* occurs in the New Testament only in Mark. The word comes from the Hebrew term meaning *offering*. It means that a man could dedicate property to God as a way to avoid his responsibility to provide for his elderly parents. At the same time, he could retain the use of the property during his lifetime. This allowed him to use his property while also claiming that he had no money to support his elderly parents, because he had dedicated it all to God.

Jesus is condemning this practice as a legalistic loophole. Corban allowed a man to circumvent the commandment to honor his parents by providing for their financial support. This continues the emphasis in the teaching of Jesus on care for the most vulnerable in the society and is consistent with his kingdom of God campaign.

Chapter 16
The Poor Widow

The Poor Widow
Mark 12:38-44

And in his teaching he said, "Beware of the scribes, who like to go about in long robes, and to have salutations in the market places and the best seats in the synagogues and the places of honor at feasts, who devour widows' houses and for a pretense make long prayers. They will receive the greater condemnation." And he sat down opposite the treasury, and watched the multitude putting money into the treasury. Many rich people put in large sums. And a poor widow came, and put in two copper coins, which make a penny. And he called his disciples to him, and said to them, "Truly, I say to you, this poor widow has put in more than all those who are contributing to the treasury. For they all contributed out of their abundance; but she out of her poverty has put in everything she had, her whole living" (Mark 12:38-44, Revised Standard Version).

The Poor Widow
Luke 20:45-47; 21:1-4

And in the hearing of all the people he said to his disciples, "Beware of the scribes, who like to go about in long robes, and love salutations in the market places and the best seats in the synagogues and the places of honor at feasts, who devour

> widows' houses and for a pretense make long
> prayers. They will receive the greater
> condemnation." He looked up and saw the rich
> putting their gifts into the treasury; and he saw a
> poor widow put in two copper coins. And he said,
> "Truly I tell you, this poor widow has put in more
> than all of them; for they all contributed out of their
> abundance, but she out of her poverty put in all the
> living that she had (Luke 20:45-47; 21:1-4, Revised
> Standard Version).

This story of the poor widow who gave away all she had to live on demonstrates the pernicious effect of biblical urban legends on the most vulnerable.

In this story, Jesus uses the widow as an example of the abuse of power by religious authorities. By disconnecting the words of Jesus about the widow from the larger context, this story about the abuse of power gets turned upside down. Before we get to the story of the widow, let's take a side trip and consider the system of dividing the Bible into chapters and verses.

The Earliest Gospel Manuscripts

When the gospels were written down, they were written in *Common Greek* in a predominantly illiterate society. Scribes were among the very few in the society who could read and write.

Written Greek had no system of punctuation. Also, papyrus was so expensive that the scribes used every bit of the paper. They didn't leave spaces between words. If they came to the edge of the paper without finishing a word, they simply continued the word on the next line. The earliest manuscripts were written exclusively in capital letters *(uncials)*. Later Greek manuscripts were written entirely in small letters *(miniscules)*. Here is what such a manuscript might look like written in capital letters:

WHENTHEGOSPELSWEREWRITTENDOWNTHEYWERE
WRITTENINCOMMONGREEKINAPREDOMINANTLYILLI
TERATESOCIETYSCRIBESWEREAMONGTHEVERYFEWI
NTHESOCIETYWHOCOULDREADANDWRITEWRITTEN
GREEKHADNOSYSTEMOFPUNCTUATIONALSOPAPYRU
SWASSOEXPENSIVETHATTHESCRIBESUSEDEVERYBITO
FTHPAPERTHEYDIDNTLEAVESPACESBETWEENWORDS
IFTHEYCAMETOTHEEDGEOFTHEPAPERWITHOUTFINIS
HINGAWORDTHEYSIMPLYCONTINUEDTHEWORDONT
OTHENEXTLINETHEEARLIESTMANUSCRIPTSWEREWRI
TTENEXCLUSIVELYINCAPITALLETTERSUNCIALSLATERG
REEKMANUSCRIPTSWEREWRITTENENTIRELYINSMALL
LETTERMINISCULESHEREISWHATSUCHAMANUSCRIPT
MIGHTLOOKLIKEWRITTENINCAPITALLETTERS

No Punctuation and No Spaces

The earliest available written manuscripts look just like this except they were handwritten with Greek characters. There were no periods, no commas, no question marks, no colons, no semi-colons, and no spaces between words. The entire system that we use in English to separate words with spaces, capitalize proper names, and to punctuate paragraphs, sentences, and phrases did not exist.

Chapters, Verses, and Punctuation in English Bibles

Any time you read an English Bible—no matter what the translation—and see sentences, paragraphs, and punctuation, all marked with chapters and verses, understand that every division was added at some point by someone much later than the original document was written who may or may not have divided up the story very well. Every time someone divides up a narrative, a story, or a speech, the division separates elements that were originally part of an undivided whole.

Nothing causes more misunderstanding of Bible stories than artificial distinctions that leave out punchlines, leave out important elements of the story, and separate what was all part of a single story to create a system of chapters, verses, and paragraphs.

The *King James Version* treated every verse as a separate paragraph. Other translations break up the narrative into paragraphs depending on how the translators understand the story elements. As a tiny effort to counteract the effect of using chapters and verses to break up stories, I have taken out the verse numbers from quoted stories in an effort to treat them as whole units rather than discrete verses.

Why the Scribes Belong in the Widow's Story

Of all of the money stories in this book, this story about the poor widow is the one where chapter and verse divisions do the most to obscure the meaning. At least in Mark, the comments about the scribes who devour widows' houses are in the same chapter as the comments about the poor widow. In Luke, they are in separate chapters, making it seem as if they are unrelated topics.

In fact, the scribes are an essential part of the story about the widow. Without the scribes, it becomes a story about a widow giving away everything she had to live on as an example of how Christians ought to give. With the scribes, it becomes an explanation of why the widow was so poor that she has only the two smallest coins, the bronze *leptas*.

Widows in Ancient Palestine

Previously, I described the basic social unit of the society. Most people lived in patriarchal family units on hereditary family land, under the authority of the ruling adult male. Women lived under the authority and protection of men. Unmarried women remained at home under the authority of their fathers. Married women lived under the authority and protection of their husbands.

While some widows in Palestine were citizens of Rome with greater legal and financial resources, most widows were extremely vulnerable. Most widows had no legal standing and no resources of their own. For this reason, the Torah always recognized widows as a special class of people who needed protection.

Devouring the Widows' Houses

In both Mark and Luke, the story of the poor widow comes immediately after Jesus condemns the practices of the scribes. The scribes were the legal scholars. They were the experts on the oral and written Torah. In both Mark and Luke, Jesus comments on the poor widow after describing the scribes as those who "devour the houses of widows."

Unless she was a Roman citizen, a widow had no legal status to manage the property and money her husband left behind. After a man's death, the scribes would appoint a "pious" man to handle the widow's financial affairs. The implication of the narrative is that the scribes used their status as experts in the law to defraud the widows out of their property. The scribes who were supposed to protect her had left her with only two tiny coins to live on.

Jesus also comments on the ostentatious giving of the rich. The rich put large sums of money into the temple treasury. Once again, it's important to pay attention to the reality that the rich got that way through the exploitation of the rest of the population.

The Outlaw Hero Version of the Widow's Story

This story is consistent with Jesus and his outlaw hero's campaign. He condemns the religious system that defrauded the poor widows and the practices of the rich because of their exploitation of the poor. He compares the contributions of the rich with the tiny contribution of the widow as a way to criticize the rich. Although the very rich gave large sums of money, what they gave made no difference in the way they lived. They gave out of their abundance. However, she gave all she had to live on.

Biblical Urban Legends about
"The Widow Who Gave Away All She Had to Live On"

Christian tradition—aided and abetted by translations that treat the story of the widow as a discrete unit—often turns this story into biblical urban legends that claim that God wants you to give away everything you have.

This story has particular meaning for me. When I went to Sunday School, the major topic of many of our opening exercises was raising money for the poor. We made little church-shaped cardboard boxes to hold our nickels and dimes so that we could help buy chickens or a cow for people in some poor village somewhere. Every Thanksgiving, we were supposed to collect food for the poor. So we brought in cans of green beans and boxes of Jell-O to donate to the poor. We heard many times about the poor widow who gave everything she had to live on as an example of what God wanted us to do.

The reality of my young life was that I was growing up in an abusive family situation and was almost always hungry, filthy, dressed in torn and dirty clothes, and feeling terrified. Every Sunday morning I got up in my unheated, uninsulated, Massachusetts bedroom, picked up dirty clothing from the floor, and got dressed. I then inched slowly, with my heart pounding, down the hallway to go out to the kitchen. My goal was to creep past the raging giant who spent Saturday and Sunday mornings in bed, sleeping it off, usually well past noon, without provoking him to bellow profanities about "stomping up and down the hall."

In the kitchen, my mother doled out nickels for the Sunday School offering. I had a brother three years older and a brother two years older. They were known throughout our childhood as a collective unit called, "The Boys." With our nickels in hand, the three of us left the house and walked to Sunday School. We never ate breakfast. In our family, breakfast was not to be "wasted" on children. In my father's opinion, he was the only one who deserved to eat breakfast since he was the only one who worked. Since going to public school and Sunday school didn't count as work, we children didn't deserve to eat breakfast. And so, we didn't.

Each week, I obediently put my nickel in the offering because God wanted me to give everything I had to the poor just as the poor widow did. My brothers were wiser than I, or maybe not as scared into submissive "goodness." They kept their nickels.

After Sunday School each week, we stopped at the drugstore to pick up the Sunday paper. While we were there, my brothers bought candy bars with their Sunday School nickels. In those days, a full-size candy bar cost a nickel. As we walked home, The Boys ate their candy bars with exaggerated enjoyment as they teased me endlessly about how they had candy and I didn't, telling me how wonderful the candy bars were.

Finally, one week, I kept my nickel when the offering basket was passed around. At the drug store, I bought a Milky Way—a monumental purchase for a child who never had any spending money. I ate about three bites of the candy bar. By the time we reached the field across from Brooks Park, I was feeling so guilty about not putting my nickel into the offering that I threw the rest of the candy bar into the field. After that, I always put my nickel into the offering, knowing that the poor deserved the money, but I didn't. I was a very good little girl and I learned my Sunday School lessons very well.

This is the essence of a biblical urban legend. I was taught Bible verses that kept me scared, obedient, and very hungry. Sunday School convinced me that God wanted me to give away my nickel to those who needed it more than I did. No one ever seemed to notice that I was a very hungry, dirty, and terrified child.

The Words in Context

When the verses are put back into the context of the whole story of Jesus—the outlaw hero on a campaign to proclaim the kingdom of God for the benefit of the poorest and most vulnerable—this story does not teach the most vulnerable of the society to give away everything they have. This is a condemnation of a religious system that robbed widows of their money.

What Sunday School taught me about this story was the worst kind of biblical urban legend. It turns a condemnation of the abuse of power into a commandment that the most vulnerable must obey authority. It distorts the point of the original story and creates fear and lack in the ones Jesus intended to liberate.

Chapter 17
The Rich Young Man

The Rich Young Man
Mark 10:17-31

And as he was setting out on his journey, a man ran up and knelt before him, and asked him, "Good Teacher, what must I do to inherit eternal life?" And Jesus said to him, "Why do you call me good? No one is good but God alone. You know the commandments: Do not kill, Do not commit adultery, Do not steal, Do not bear false witness, Do not defraud, Honor your father and mother.'" And he said to him, "Teacher, all these I have observed from my youth." And Jesus looking upon him loved him, and said to him, "You lack one thing; go, sell what you have, and give to the poor, and you will have treasure in heaven; and come, follow me." At that saying his countenance fell, and he went away sorrowful; for he had great possessions. And Jesus looked around and said to his disciples, "How hard it will be for those who have riches to enter the kingdom of God!" And the disciples were amazed at his words. But Jesus said to them again, "Children, how hard it is to enter the kingdom of God! It is easier for a camel to go through the eye of a needle than for a rich man to enter the kingdom of God." And they were exceedingly astonished, and said to him, "Then who can be saved?" Jesus looked at them and said, "With men it is impossible, but not with God; for all things are possible with God." Peter began to say to him, "Lo, we have left everything and followed you." Jesus said, "Truly, I say to you, there is no one who has left house or brothers or sisters or mother or father or children or lands, for my sake and for the gospel, who will not receive a hundredfold now in this time, houses and brothers and sisters and mothers and children and lands, with persecutions, and in the age to come eternal life. But many that are first will be last, and the last first" (Mark 10:17-31, Revised Standard Version).

The Rich Young Man
Matthew 19:16-30

And behold, one came up to him, saying, "Teacher, what good deed must I do, to have eternal life?" And he said to him, "Why do you ask me about what is good? One there is who is good. If you would enter life, keep the commandments." He said to him, "Which?" And Jesus said, "You shall not kill, You shall not commit adultery, You shall not steal, You shall not bear false witness, Honor your father and mother, and, You shall love your neighbor as yourself." The young man said to him, "All these I have observed; what do I still lack?" Jesus said to him, "If you would be perfect, go, sell what you possess and give to the poor, and you will have treasure in heaven; and come, follow me." When the young man heard this he went away sorrowful; for he had great possessions. And Jesus said to his disciples, "Truly, I say to you, it will be hard for a rich man to enter the kingdom of heaven. Again I tell you, it is easier for a camel to go through the eye of a needle than for a rich man to enter the kingdom of God." When the disciples heard this they were greatly astonished, saying, "Who then can be saved?" But Jesus looked at them and said to them, "With men this is impossible, but with God all things are possible." Then Peter said in reply, "Lo, we have left everything and followed you. What then shall we have?" Jesus said to them, "Truly, I say to you, in the new world, when the Son of man shall sit on his glorious throne, you who have followed me will also sit on twelve thrones, judging the twelve tribes of Israel. And every one who has left houses or brothers or sisters or father or mother or children or lands, for my name's sake, will receive a hundredfold, and inherit eternal life. But many that are first will be last, and the last first" (Matthew 19:16-30, Revised Standard Version).

The Rich Young Man
Luke 18:18-30

And a ruler asked him, "Good Teacher, what shall I do to inherit eternal life?" And Jesus said to him, "Why do you call me good? No one is good but God alone. You know the commandments: Do not commit adultery, Do not kill, Do not steal, Do not bear false witness, Honor your father and mother.'" And he said, "All these I have observed from my youth." And when Jesus heard it, he said to him, "One thing you still lack. Sell all that you have and distribute to the poor, and you will have treasure in heaven; and come, follow me." But when he heard this he became sad, for he was very rich. Jesus looking at him said, "How hard it is for those who have riches to enter the kingdom of God! For it is easier for a camel to go through the eye of a needle than for a rich man to enter the kingdom of God." Those who heard it said, "Then who can be saved?" But he said, "What is impossible with men is possible with God." And Peter said, "Lo, we have left our homes and followed you." And he said to them, "Truly, I say to you, there is no man who has left house or wife or brothers or parents or children, for the sake of the kingdom of God, ho will not receive manifold more in this time, and in the age to come eternal life" (Luke 18:18-30, Revised Standard Version).

Exaggerated Metaphors

It's time to come back to the place we started to the story of the rich young man. We've come a long way from the question the student asked at the seminar: "How can you say it is good to be rich when Jesus said that a rich man can't get into heaven?" By now, it ought to be clear that there was no gate in Jerusalem called the Eye of the Needle. The reference to a camel and the eye of a needle was exaggerated metaphorical language. Jesus spoke often in exaggerated metaphors, such as the one about having a log in your eye:

> Why do you see the speck that is in your brother's eye, but do not notice the log that is in your own eye? (Matthew 7:3, Revised Standard Version).

We have looked at what Jesus said about money to his disciples and his enemies, about disciples, beggars, and a poor widow. Now we return to the top of the social order.

Putting the Rich Young Man into His Context

Before we assume that Jesus is making a statement about all rich people in all times and places, we need to be clear about what he is saying to one particular rich man in a particular time and place.

In an agrarian society, a rich person was rich because he was the beneficiary of a social system that left the vast majority of the population living in poverty. The problem with the rich young man was not the fact that he was rich. The problem was that his wealth derived from an economic system of exploitation, oppression, and injustice.

From Salvation to the kingdom of God

The young man asks about his own salvation. Jesus moves the question beyond personal salvation to the vision of the kingdom of God. When Jesus says that the rich cannot enter the kingdom of God he is not talking about an afterlife. And he's not saying that if you have money, you can't get into heaven. He is talking about the overthrow of the existing order of things in which those who are rich and at the top of the social system will lose their advantage.

To enter the kingdom of God, the rich need to see beyond their own sense of privilege. They need to see that all human beings deserve to live lives of abundance. When Jesus tells the rich young ruler to give away his possessions to the poor, he is challenging the rich young man on this point. To give his money to the poor is to return what he had gained through an oppressive economic system.

The Call to Discipleship

The most significant aspect of this story is that Jesus is calling the young man to discipleship. He is asking the rich young man to do what he asks of every other disciple: "Leave everything and follow me." He isn't creating a special set of conditions for the rich young man. He demands this of all of his followers.

Call to a Hero's Journey

Jesus calls the rich man to his own hero's journey. For the rich young man to follow Jesus, he would have to undergo the same steps that every hero undergoes. He would have to accept the call to adventure, leave his ordinary world, and set out on a journey to follow Jesus.

Rather than see Jesus' comment about the rich man and the eye of the needle as a condemnation of being rich, it is more instructive to see it as a commentary on the young man's refusal of the invitation to be a disciple—to refuse the call to be a hero.

Refusing the Call

In his excellent book about the hero's journey, *Stealing Fire From The Gods*, James Bonnet identifies the *holdfast* as the one who resists change. He claims:

> In great stories, ninety-nine out of a hundred heroes take up the challenge. In real life, the vast majority refuse. To refuse the call means to let the problems slide and not become part of the solution. The world remains in trouble and we remain stuck (Bonnet 128).

In this story, the rich young man refuses the call. It's also significant to note the reactions of the bystanders. They are amazed at the idea that a rich man cannot enter the kingdom of God. They are expressing the belief that wealth is a sign of blessing. If the rich cannot be saved, who can?

The Point of the Story in Another Context

What is the point of this story for those of us who live in a different economic and political system? Ethically and spiritually, the point is the same. Each of us has choices about money. Wealth can be gained and used unjustly. Wealth can also be gained and used justly and with great benefit for others.

When Jesus says that it is easier for a camel to go through the eye of a needle than for a rich person to enter the kingdom of God, he is not condemning wealth.

He is making a comment about the worldview and mentality of a rich person who has been the beneficiary of a social system that leaves most people impoverished. He is making a comment about how difficult it is for people of great wealth to change their attitudes toward everyone else.

The reason the rich young man walks away is that he cannot imagine himself as anything except the privileged rich at the top of the social system. The infamous statement by Leona Helmsley gets to the heart of the matter. When she said, "Only the little people pay taxes," she was setting herself apart from "the little people."

By putting the words of Jesus into his own social context and into the context of what he meant by the kingdom of God, we have an entirely new way to understand these words.

What does this mean for us? Even though we live in an advanced capitalistic society, we too live in a society with great inequities in wealth. Much of our society's wealth is also concentrated in the hands of few and our society also knows about oppression and exploitation by the rich. However, unlike the agrarian society in which Jesus lived, our economy allows people to create wealth without exploiting other people.

We have models in our economic system of extremely wealthy people using their riches to benefit other people. As an example, consider Bill Gates. A lot of people hate Bill Gates and anything related to Microsoft. The relevant point is that Bill Gates amassed a vast fortune through Microsoft products. At one point, he was the richest man in the world.

In many ways, using Bill Gates as an example raises many ethical questions about how he acquired his wealth. Although these are valid questions, I use Bill Gates as a prime example about the use of great wealth as a force for social change.

In the second half of his life, Gates is following the Andrew Carnegie model of expending his fortune for the benefit of humanity. Gates has decided to use his enormous financial resources to eradicate malaria in Africa. Many generations before AIDS, malaria was the scourge of Africa. The Gates Foundation is pouring millions of dollars into research on vaccines and medical training to end malaria and AIDS in Africa. Whether or not his efforts succeed, he is providing a model of using great wealth to benefit the poor rather than to oppress them.

Part Five

What

The Money Stories

Mean

For You

Chapter 18
Money Is Power

What I have done with these three gospels is equivalent to skipping a rock over the surface of a lake. Even though I have barely touched the surface at a few points, each particular story is simply one more surface mushroom connected to the giant mushroom lying beneath the surface. The mushroom underneath the three synoptic gospels is the power structure in an advanced agrarian society. The three synoptic gospels describe an outlaw hero on a campaign to liberate the oppressed from a religious and political system that concentrates wealth and blessing for the benefit of the powerful while most people suffer terrible deprivation.

Missing the Intention of the Stories

What is profoundly disturbing to me is that this real intention is so seldom taught in Sunday Schools and churches. Instead, these stories of the outlaw hero's attempt to set people free from economic and religious abuse get turned into biblical urban legends warning people about the evils of money.

Consider the story of the poor widow. Who could possibly be poorer than a widow in ancient Jerusalem who had two tiny coins? What kind of religious teaching would convince such a woman to give away to the temple all that she has to live on? It's the same religious teaching that attacked me with guilt when I threw away a candy bar bought with the nickel I was supposed to give to the church to feed faraway people whose hunger was more important than mine.

Bad Teaching

The old adage says: "If you're a hammer, everything looks like a nail." I am a teacher. To this teacher, it all comes down to bad teaching. It starts with extracting Bible verses from whole stories and turning them into rules to live by, without paying attention to the real intention behind the stories. Bad teaching separates the stories from the social context and treats them as if history, geography, and sociology don't matter.

As a result of ignoring these contexts of gospel story and agrarian society, the type of people Jesus intended to liberate are often the ones who feel the greatest guilt about money.

From my current vantage point as a person who spent many years of my adult life in rigorous academic study of the Bible, I see clearly that Jesus was the outlaw hero. The core of his message was an assault on the abuse of power by those in authority, the abuse of power that kept most people struggling, hungry, suffering, and broke.

As a teacher and biblical scholar, I look at these gospels now and wonder: How is it that almost everything I was taught in church was so backwards, upside down, turned on its head? How they could have so completely turned good news into bad news? How could they turn *Liberating Bible* into *Constraining Bible?*

Using the Stories to Teach Obedience

The dominant theme of my own Christian education was obedience. Even as an abused child, I learned very early that my role mattered more than my wellbeing as a person. My entire religious obligation was summed up in the phrase: Be obedient to authority.

From my vantage point, years after my earliest Bible lessons in Sunday School, I look back at what I was taught and I ponder:

> Why was I taught so much about obedience to authority?
>
> Why was I taught that God wanted me to be poor?
>
> Why was I taught that God wanted me to give away anything I had?
>
> Why was I taught to be silent?
>
> Why was I taught that I had no right to be angry about anything?

In short, why was I taught that God wanted me powerless, silent, passive, and broke? Why was I taught *Constraining Bible* instead of *Liberating Bible?*

While I was teaching seminary students—who were going to become pastors, ministers, and priests—I had them look carefully at the lectionary readings chosen from whatever biblical book we were studying. Many Christian churches use a lectionary containing a three-year cycle of readings, with an Old Testament reading, a reading from the New Testament letters, and a gospel reading. I asked my students to look at the lectionary readings and consider whether the readings chosen for church services were an accurate representation of the whole book. What topics were chosen? What topics were left out?

As a teacher, I observed many times that if I asked my students a real question, without expecting a particular answer, they would often reach profound insights. They would tell me how the lectionary readings so often skewed meaning.

What is most striking to me is that few lectionary readings address the abuse of power by people in authority, which is a dominant theme in the synoptic gospels.

Who Benefits?

One of my favorite outlaw questions is: *Who benefits from this?* Who benefits from a system of religious education that teaches people to obey rules without teaching that Jesus was the outlaw hero who died because he challenged a religious and economic system that taught that the rich deserved to be rich and the poor deserved to be poor?

In the synoptic gospels, the kingdom of God is about a reordering of power, but I was taught that I had to obey whoever had power over me.

What I Never Learned in Sunday School

I never remember hearing anyone talk about the saying of Jesus:

> "Whoever receives one such child in my name receives me; but whoever causes one of these little ones who believe in me to sin, it would be better for him to have a great millstone fastened round his neck and to be drowned in the depth of the sea" (Matthew 18: 5-6, Revised Standard Version).

This Bible quotation deserves particular comment. In my first version of this book, I cited this quotation without challenging the translation itself.

However, Matthew 18 is the focal point of my book, *Your True Self Identity: How Familiar Translations of Bible Verses in the Gospel of Matthew Hide Your True Identity from You.*

The central topic of the book is the effect of sin theology on identity. My claim is that any translation that refers to *little ones* as *sinners* has significantly mistranslated the Greek text and has profoundly distorted the meaning of Matthew in Chapter 18. In fact, Matthew 18:6 focuses on those who abuse their power and does not say that little ones *sin*.

Matthew 18:1-14 in Greek is a clear condemnation of the abuse of the vulnerable by those with power, which is consistent with the gospel stories about the outlaw hero Jesus. The translations turn the little ones into sinners. Despite the overwhelming focus of the Christian gospels on the abuse of the vulnerable by the powerful, I don't remember ever hearing a Sunday School lesson or a church sermon about the words of Jesus that challenged the power of the rulers:

> But Jesus called them to him and said, "You know that the rulers of the Gentiles lord it over them, and their great men exercise authority over them. It shall not be so among you; but whoever would be great among you must be your servant, and whoever would be first among you must be your slave; even as the Son of man came not to be served but to serve, and to give his life as a ransom for many" (Matthew 20:25-28, Revised Standard Version).

Instead, I heard many lessons about obedience to authority and the sin of pride. Why did my Sunday School teach me to be broke? For the same reason they wanted me to be obedient. Obedient, broke people don't rock the boat.

My Sunday School teachers aren't at fault here. Most were well-meaning volunteers with absolutely no training in Bible. They were simply teaching the lessons in the lesson books, doing what they were told.

Leading the Sheep

Another misunderstood metaphor of the Christian church concerns shepherds and sheep. Jesus is the good shepherd who cares for the sheep. He seeks the lost sheep and brings them safely home.

In the church, the language of shepherd and sheep can very easily take on a disturbing connotation. Churches use this "shepherd and sheep" language to distinguish between the leaders and the led. *Pastor* is Latin for *shepherd* and the people become the sheep of the flock. Sheep are not known for their independence. With this language, the ones cared for become the ones to be led. When my well-meaning Sunday school teachers taught me to be obedient to authority, it was a case of sheep teaching other sheep how to be better sheep.

Significantly, Matthew 18:1-14 also includes the parable of the "lost sheep." English translations consistently identify the little ones as sinners who go astray. In fact, the Greek is very clear that the little ones do not go astray. Instead they are led astray.

The reality is that there is tremendous vested interest in political and religious institutions to teach people to surrender both money and power to authority.

St. Petersburg

When I visited St. Petersburg, Russia while my husband was part of a men's chorus on tour, I understood why the Russian revolution started in St. Petersburg. Everywhere we went, we toured palaces and churches—decaying monuments to the idea that wealth is a sign of God's blessing. St. Petersburg was built on the delta of the Neva River at the far end of the Baltic Sea, as a grand monument to Peter the Great. Thousands of conscripted workers died to build the palaces, churches, and canals in the swamps of the Neva to glorify the king.

This is what kings do. This is what kings have always done. They build elaborate palaces and churches and tombs, using the forced labor of the people, as visible symbols of divine blessing. From the pyramids in Egypt, to the Taj Mahal in India, and the great palaces and cathedrals of Europe, kings will bankrupt a society to demonstrate that the gods have blessed the rule of the monarch.

Kings and Patriarchs

For this reason, it is dubious justification for Christians to adopt a theology that claims that God is going to bless you with material wealth by citing examples of the kings and patriarchs.

In the Old Testament, Solomon is the quintessential king in an agrarian society. He builds a grand temple and a grand palace using conscripted labor as proof that God has chosen him as the king (1 Kings 5-9).

It costs money to build such monuments. It still costs money to build and maintain elaborate churches and to pay for the shepherds to lead the flocks. Unfortunately, history demonstrates that all too often the shepherds shear the sheep of their money.

In the society in which we live, money is power. We all need money. Ignorance of money is no virtue. Ignorance of money simply makes you vulnerable to the decisions of other people. How many people who thought they would retire with comfortable pensions now find that corporations have simply declared that they would not honor the pensions? How many people lost their retirement investments in the stock market when the economy teetered on the edge of ruin? How many people lost jobs and cannot find new ones? How many people lost houses because the banks rigged the system?

If I could live my life over, the single most important change I would make is that I would have studied money much, much earlier. Money is neither good nor bad. It is simply a tool. Those who learn to use it well have one of the most powerful tools for taking control of their financial lives. Those who don't know how to use money are at the mercy of others.

The Christian Money Taboo

There is no power in being ignorant of money. Yet, too often church leaders teach that knowledge of money is somehow unchristian.

I once attended a four-day seminar about creating wealth. I met many people and learned about various types of wealth-building investments. Over lunch one day, I got involved in a very serious conversation about the Bible and beliefs about money with a husband and wife who were committed members of their church. I'll call them John and Mary. During the conversation, John said something revealing. He said that he wouldn't want to tell anyone in his church that they were attending a seminar about creating wealth.

I have met so many people like John and Mary. They are good, loving, loyal people of faith. They desire to do the right thing. They seek to live their lives in a way that is honest and honorable. They seek to serve other people. And they carry within themselves deep guilt about their own desire to have money. The question is: Why do Christian people of faith have to hide the truth that they are going to attend a seminar about creating wealth?

The Wrong Question

Let's return to the question posed by Time Magazine: "Does God want you to be rich?" The question itself is flawed. It makes money only a personal matter.

I am also very aware that the subtitle I chose for this book also makes money a personal matter. It's another question focused on you and your money: *How Do Bible Verses about Jesus, Wealth, Poverty and Heaven Affect Your Income?*

Why did I choose this subtitle, knowing very well that anyone who has read this far and grasped the central point of *Gospel of Wealth or Poverty?* has every reason to challenge me on this choice?

I posed the question in personal terms for the same reason that Time made its question personal. Most of us who write with the hope that other people will read what we write have been persuaded that the only way to get someone's attention these days is to make it personal. In other words, I wanted you to read my book.

Marketers refer to *WIIFM*. This acronym claims that everyone is walking around tuned into an imaginary radio station with the call letters WIIFM—letters that stand for *what's in it for me?*

Ask yourself if you would read a book with a subtitle that read something like: *How Do Bible Verses about Jesus, Wealth, Poverty and Heaven Increase the Wealth of the Rich and the Poverty of the Poor?*

As a former academic, I can tell you that this is the kind of title that academics put on scholarly papers and books. It's the kind of writing that other academics read that seems completely irrelevant to non-academics.

Be honest with yourself. Would you be interested in such broad categories without any reference to how any if would affect you?

The Jesus portrayed in the synoptic gospels would not have asked the question this way. From the perspective of Jesus in the gospels, your income is not just about you. Your income is directly related to your social status.

On this point, the proponents of the "Social Gospel Camp" are closer to the mark than the proponents of the "Prosperity Camp." At the same time, prosperity teaching is a reaction against the kind of teaching I heard as a child. It's a reaction against those who taught John and Mary that they should not attend a seminar about creating wealth.

The significant problem is that we have two positions, both basing their arguments on Bible verses. The

"Prosperity Camp" argues for personal wealth without paying much attention to the injustices of the social structure. The "Social Gospel Camp" argues against the injustices of the social structure while expressing great suspicion of personal wealth.

The Time magazine article is another case of skipping stones across a lake. To address the issues raised in this one article, I would need to write another book. I offer only these observations.

In an article asking the question: "Does God want you to be rich," no one refers to the kingdom of God, which is the foundational concept of the synoptic gospels. They refer to the riches of heaven, but not to the kingdom of heaven. They refer to wealth without examining money. They refer to social justice without referring to power.

Is this because the experts didn't talk about these matters? Is it because the authors didn't include any comments the experts made on these topics? The nature of the article itself is the equivalent of "verses versus verses." Time included a few Bible verses and a few comments from several scholars and pastors without putting their comments into their own contexts.

It's also a case of collecting a few comments without paying sufficient attention to the religious, social, and economic contexts of contemporary America.

The result is a series of disconnected comments from several people about Bible verses. How can such an article even begin to address the complexities of the question?

A Difficult Book

I can't imagine a more difficult book than the Bible. The word *Bible* means *books* in Greek. The Bible is a collection of books, not a single book. If the Bible were just a collection of books, it would be hard enough to sort through the layers of composition, language, and history to understand what it all meant.

As Holy Scripture, the Bible gains an additional layer of complexity. Now the collection of books becomes one book, a book that is both fully divine and fully human. Reading the Bible as Holy Scripture becomes even more complicated, laden with conflicting opinions about inspiration, inerrancy, and infallibility.

The Bible as "The Word of God"

The Bible becomes infinitely more difficult when it is identified as *The Word of God*.

Consider the implications of this language. Many books turn into one Book. Many words turn into one Word. The particular becomes the Universal. Truths become one Truth.

The singularity of *The Word of God* collapses all distinctions of time, space, language, and social status into a singular book identified as "The Word." Fundamentalists and evangelicals take it one step further to claim that the Bible is inerrant and infallible. There can be no contradictions and no errors. The Bible as the *inerrant, infallible Word of God* conveys the singular truth about any topic.

This is the ultimate constriction. In such a view of the Bible, there's no room for complexity of vision. The singular allows only one truth about anything. Choose one side or the other. There can be no multiplicity of meanings, no doubt, no confusion. Complexity turns into the dogmatic simplicity of either/or.

Despite this reduction of the many to the one, this is what I know to be true. The Bible is simply too complicated to make any kind of coherent universal doctrine of money based on a few isolated Bible verses, and then to apply this doctrine to any and all situations as if particularity of context doesn't matter.

Bible Stories as Rhetoric

At this point, I would like to make a case for the extraordinary insights of rhetoric. Rhetoric is the study of persuasive speech. It originated with Aristotle in ancient Athens. Rhetoric was further developed and expanded in ancient Rome, especially by Cicero. For more than a thousand years of Western history, rhetoric was the foundation of education.

The fundamental insight of rhetoric applied to the Bible is that the gospels were written to persuade particular audiences about a particular point of view.

Did Jesus Preach a Gospel of Wealth?

You have to look hard in the synoptic gospels to make a case that Jesus is preaching a gospel of wealth. If you narrow your focus enough, you can cite the Bible verses that Time cites as evidence that God wants you to be rich:

> The thief comes only to steal and kill and destroy; I came that they may have life, and have it abundantly (John 10:10, Revised Standard Version).

> ...give and it will be given to you; good measure, pressed down, shaken together, running over, will be put into your lap. For the measure you give will be the measure you get back" (Luke 6:38, Revised Standard Version).

These are fragments, which come in the context of Jesus' comments about judgment and forgiveness.

The quotation from John is significant, since the promise of *abundant life* is an important theme in the gospel of John. Whether this means that Jesus wants you to be rich is another matter. Although neither of these verses explicitly mentions money, you can claim that Jesus wants you to have abundant wealth but it's hard to make a compelling case from these two verses.

You have to ignore just about everything else in the New Testament gospel stories to make the case that Jesus is preaching a gospel of wealth.

Why didn't Jesus make a stronger case for wealth? It's the same reason that no one would teach a starving person how to go on a weight loss diet. Jesus had enough to do to claim that even the poor were included in God's blessing. He wasn't attempting to teach the poor how to become rich.

Earlier, I asked another question: Why is it that the United States of America, which is a predominantly Christian society, has the same division of wealth as almost every other society? Why is it that a handful of rich people control most of the money? Why do so many honest, hardworking Christian people struggle so much with money? Why do so many people in the richest society on earth go broke?

My answer is that the stories about an outlaw hero turned into biblical urban legends. The solution is to recover the hero's story and resolve to set out on a hero's journey about money.

Chapter 19
Your Heroic Money Journey

Each of us is a storyteller. How you live your life doesn't depend only on the facts of your life—where you live, your occupation, your age, gender, or social status. It also depends on the stories you tell yourself about your life.

This is a book about two types of stories about money: the biblical urban legend and the hero's journey.

Biblical Urban Legends

The first type of story is what I call a biblical urban legend. These stories usually start with a kernel of truth but become embellished and distorted with the telling and retelling. The fundamental difference between a hero's journey and a biblical urban legend is not the content of the story itself but the effect on the hearers. They have the same effect as ghost stories around the campfire. Biblical urban legends warn of lurking dangers. They create fear of taking action in the big, bad world out there. They teach you to be fearful in the face of injustice, passive in the face of threat, and concerned with self-preservation in the face of danger to yourself and others.

In short, a biblical urban legend warns people to stay at home in your ordinary world, with your doors and windows locked. Don't act. Don't challenge. Don't confront. Be safe.

The Hero's Journey

The second type of story is the hero's journey. This type of story has been with us as long as human beings have been able to speak of their fears, their hopes, their dreams, and their struggles. This is the kind of story told around campfires to inspire, thrill, and encourage. Joseph Campbell identified the form and gave it a name but the hero's journey has been with us forever.

In its most basic form, the hero is anyone—male or female—who perceives that something is wrong in the hero's world. This is the threat. The hero chooses to act to solve the problem, motivated by a sense of responsibility to restore the hero's world to its balance. Usually the decision to act requires the hero to overcome initial reluctance.

The journey requires the hero to leave what is ordinary and familiar to set out into a special and unfamiliar world. Along the way, the hero meets mentors who provide gifts for the task, as well as allies and adversaries. Finally the hero must come face to face with the ultimate cause of the threat. On the way, the hero must act in spite of fear, persevere in the face of all obstacles, and do whatever is required to accomplish the task. If the hero defeats the adversary, the hero returns to the hero's ordinary world. While the hero's actions solve the problem for the benefit of the hero's ordinary world, the hero is forever changed as a result of the journey.

In short, the hero chooses to act in the face of fear, persist in the face of obstacles, and confront the real source of the threat for some larger purpose than the hero's own benefit.

What It Means

Earlier, I defined exegesis as the effort to determine *what it meant* and hermeneutics as *what it means*. Although no one is ever truly neutral about anything, responsible exegetes at least consciously attempt to separate out their own theological beliefs and opinions in an effort to determine what the biblical authors intended. This is what I have attempted to do in this book in an effort to read the stories without imposing my own religious beliefs upon them.

Hermeneutics brings a new word into the picture: *belief*. Whatever you believe about the words of Jesus—"infallible, inerrant, inspired words of God," or ignorant superstition, or any other description—*what it means* depends on your own beliefs about God, Jesus, and the Bible.

Whatever your own beliefs, the gospel stories about Jesus are bona fide hero's journeys. In the gospels of Matthew, Mark, and Luke, Jesus acts heroically and goes to Jerusalem to face the threat in the ordinary world—the political and religious power structure that created such suffering and hardship for the majority of the people.

Stories in Christian Tradition

Whatever else Christian tradition has done, it has told the story of Jesus for almost two thousand years. My question is this: Has Christian tradition told the story as a hero's journey or as a biblical urban legend? Clearly, the correct answer is: both.

The underlying premise of this book is that many of the stories told about Jesus and money are not told as hero's stories. Instead, they are told as biblical urban legends.

This seems particularly true with stories about money. On the whole, the church has been telling the wrong story about money. The dominant tendency of the Christian church has been to turn whatever Jesus said about money as part of the hero's story into biblical urban legends warning about the dangers of being rich. Too often the retold stories about Jesus on the topic of money are not heroic stories but cautionary tales. They do not inspire people to face their fears and go out into the world to resolve the problem created by the threat. Instead, they are stories told to create fear, guilt, and limitation.

The prevailing biblical urban legend about money goes something like this:

> Jesus taught people that money is bad. If you have any, give it away. Jesus wants you to be broke, to prove that you love God more than money.

As a call to action, there is nothing heroic about this story. Nothing that is going to stir anyone to action. Nothing that will inspire you with a burning conviction that you must do something to make the world a better place.

The Prosperity Camp and the Hero's Journey

Let's go back to the dichotomy posed by the two sides of the Prosperity Camp. There is something compelling on the prosperity side in the idea that Christians are going to stop living their lives according to biblical urban legends that God wants you to be broke.

Yet, I have rarely encountered people who espouse a prosperity vision who connect prosperity with any larger heroic vision. I remember the first time I met people who were part of a prosperity gospel movement. They kept saying things like: "I'm a king's kid and the king wants me to travel first class. This is why I deserve a Cadillac."

From the perspective of a hero's journey, there is nothing heroic about such a statement. Nothing that addresses any imbalance in the ordinary world. Nothing that requires the speaker to face fears, obstacles, or adversaries. No elixir for anyone else.

In my opinion, if you want a Cadillac, buy a Cadillac. However, there seems to be no inherent connection between driving a Cadillac and Jesus' heroic journey to address the economic injustices of his own social system.

Poverty and the Hero's Journey

What about the idea that God wants you to serve the poor by being poor? I know a young woman who wants to be a medical missionary committed to serving the poor. She is also convinced that God wants her to be poor, which is another way of saying that she has never accepted any kind of responsibility for earning her own money. Her mother has said to her: "With your brilliance, imagine what you could accomplish with a lot of money."

But the devout young woman is convinced that God wants her to be poor. She goes through life with her hand out, expecting other people to pay her way. She feels entitled to handouts because she says she wants to serve God.

There is nothing very heroic about this attitude either. By remaining willfully ignorant of money and unwilling to do anything to provide money for herself, she surrenders her power to people with money.

These are extreme examples, but they reveal common tendencies among those who claim that wealth is a sign of God's blessing and those who claim that being poor demonstrates faith in God.

A Hero's Money Journey

The solution to the problem of money in our society cannot be found on either side of a dichotomy between personal wealth as a demonstration of God's blessing and personal poverty for the sake of social justice. What I propose is a vision of money that combines the commitment to justice with a commitment to claim personal power over money.

An Invitation

At this point, I issue my own invitation: Commit yourself to your own hero's money journey. Whatever your own experience with money, whatever you learned about money from any part of the Bible, whatever your own religious belief, whether or not you are Christian, the significant question is not whether or not God wants you to be rich or poor. The real question is: Will you be heroic about money?

I return to James Bonnet's claim that what sets story heroes apart from most of us is that the hero accepts the challenge of the hero's journey. In real life, most people do not accept the call to adventure. They choose to stay in their ordinary world, unwilling to face the challenge.

Here's what I propose. Look beyond the Bible verses—the ones that tell you that you are supposed to give away all your money and to surrender riches. Also look beyond other Bible verses—the ones that tell you that God will shower you with blessings if you tithe. Discover the hero's journey within the whole story and then set out on your own hero's journey about money.

Leave the Familiar

Your own hero's journey about money would require you to leave what is familiar and enter into a special world. For many of us, that means moving from powerlessness, helplessness, and ignorance about money into the world of financial literacy. It means to claim the power of money in a world where money is the fundamental instrument of power separating the haves and the have nots. It's no surprise that people with power want to keep other people ignorant about money. Power is money and money is power.

Justice

It would also require you to take seriously that we live in a world of extreme differences between the rich and the poor. Money is too important to be left to those who have no concern for justice.

When you have money, you have the power to have a greater impact in the world. Most of us are used to playing small roles, partly because we don't have enough money. I have been part of many churches that collected money for social causes, but the amounts were always small and the impact minimal. So many people who do choose to serve the poor constantly struggle for money.

As a hungry, scared child in Sunday school, I was taught that my nickel would make a difference in a hungry world. In fact, my nickel was a drop in the ocean. The church can't address the systemic problem of hunger in the world with the nickels of Sunday School children.

In contrast consider what money can do when you have a lot of it. When a very rich man, such as Bill Gates, decides to commit millions of dollars to a systemic approach to an endemic illness, it's the difference between small gestures and the possibility of real social change.

Why Accept a Hero's Money Journey?

Why would you accept a hero's money journey? One of the most alluring claims of our age is that money ought to come easily. We live in an era of get rich quick promises. Lotteries lure us with the dreams of striking the jackpot. "Business-In-A-Box" offers tempt us with the idea that we can rake in profits without doing any work.

Instead, the hero's journey is not easy, not quick, and has no guarantees of success. Why accept the hero's call to adventure? Jim Rohn claimed that the best reason to set a goal to become a millionaire is not because of the money, but because of the person you must become to accomplish the goal:

> Set a goal to become a millionaire for what it makes
> of you to achieve it (Jim Rohn).

In other words, when you set out on a hero's journey, the journey itself will change you.

When you make a commitment to a hero's journey about money, you are committing yourself to discovering power that you never knew you had, in service of something bolder than simply acquiring more "stuff."

In the three synoptic gospels of Matthew, Mark, and Luke, the unifying vision is the kingdom of God. It is Jesus' own mission statement, which gave him a focus and defining purpose for his life. Bill Gates has a vision of solving the problem of malaria. Your own vision could be much smaller. Or it could be a bigger vision, focused on making more than a nickel's worth of difference in this world.

Money is power. When you commit yourself to your own hero's journey about money—whatever form that will take—you can make a difference in this world divided between the haves and the have-nots. You can also make a difference in your own life, to create abundance instead of constant struggle over money.

Conclusion

After all of this, the question that remains is: So What? What does any of this mean for you in the twenty-first century?

The Preface to the Revised Edition began by stating that this book has a publication history. I wrote the first version in 2003 as an ebook. Now, eleven years later, I return to the book because the world we live in has changed since then.

The biggest difference is that the economic climate has changed dramatically. The real estate bubble burst. Ordinary people lost jobs, savings, homes, and in many cases, hope of ever recovering financial stability and security. Meanwhile, the rich got richer and the poor got poorer. The economic actions that were supposed to change everything have been handouts to big corporations and banks, "austerity" spending for social programs, and decreased taxes for the very rich. At the same time, farfetched claims about "what the Bible says" have become the grounds for economic and social policies.

Parallels between Then and Now

In other words, the more things change, the more they stay the same. The rich get richer and the poor get poorer. Anyone who has done more with the Bible than read isolated Bible verses can see parallels between the ancient world of the Bible and the contemporary world. Economic oppression is a significant theme of the Hebrew prophets. It's a primary theme of the New Testament Gospels. The rich use government and religion to consolidate their oppressive financial power over the majority. They control more and more of the wealth and in the process, drive more and more of the population into poverty, sickness, and suffering.

Meanwhile, other portions of the Bible justify the consolidation of wealth and power in the hands of the king and temple. The story of Solomon with all of his wealth is a prime example of the financial rewards of being God's chosen.

The cover story of Time magazine cited earlier demonstrates the source of the problem—the futility of choosing between either/or Bible verses. If you build your theology of money on isolated Bible verses, you can justify just about anything. You can make the case that Jesus wants you to be poor. You can also make the case that Jesus wants you to rich. But neither argument can be justified if you go beyond the verses and read whole stories set in their original social, economic, political, and religious contexts. *Contexts* is the critical word, the word that is missing in so much of what people claim about the Bible.

Translation issues and salvation doctrine are also important. In this book, I have done almost nothing with either, but these are also fundamental factors in any reading of the Bible. [*Your True Self Identity* focuses on the effect of salvation doctrine on translations.]

Beyond the Either/Or

All of this leads up to this final assertion. Whatever Jesus says about money in the New Testament cannot be the foundation of economic and social policy in the twenty-first century. However, the words of Jesus in these gospel stories are profoundly relevant for any kind of discussion about the intersection of money, political power, and religion in any society.

Consider the two options of the title: *Gospel of Wealth or Poverty?* For Carnegie—a very rich man—his "Gospel of Wealth" allowed the very rich to keep their money based on the assumption that only the very rich had the economic wisdom to administer wealth wisely for the benefit of the poor. The best that can be said for Carnegie's solution is that he wanted to use his wealth to benefit others. As a whole, Carnegie's solution reeks of paternalism and privilege as well as judgments about who is worthy to receive financial benefits.

What about the option offered by Jesus in the gospels? He offered a Gospel of Poverty: "Leave everything and follow me." On this issue, I make no effort to discuss the claims by prosperity gospel preachers that Jesus was actually rich rather than poor. These arguments are a case of missing the forest for the trees. They cite Bible verses to make their case that Jesus was rich without setting all of these words in the whole story context. In the story context, Jesus was not a wealthy man promising wealth to his followers. My purpose is not to evaluate their arguments but to point out that most Christians throughout history have believed that Jesus was calling his followers to a life of poverty.

Throughout Christian history, members of various religious orders have taken vows of poverty based on the belief that they were leaving everything and following Jesus. Vows of poverty usually mean that you expect someone else to pay your way. Money has to come from somewhere. If you don't earn enough money to buy your food, someone has to earn the money to buy your food for you. Someone has to pay to build the churches, cathedrals, and monasteries.

Although Gandhi was not Christian, consider the implications of this often quoted statement by Sarojini Naidu, one of Gandhi's supporters: "To keep Mahatma Gandhi poor, we have to destroy treasures. His poverty is very costly" (Shwetashva).

In earlier eras of human history, human beings could get along without money. They were hunter-gatherers living off the land. In remote areas of the world, some human beings still live that way. However, most of the more than seven billion people who now live on this earth need money to live. Ask the millions who live in poverty how life is for them. Consider the children who starve to death for lack of food. Consider the homeless who have no place to live. A gospel of poverty is not the answer.

The Question Mark and Your Relationship with Money

The question mark at the end of *Gospel of Wealth or Money?* is the most significant component of the title and the most easily overlooked. It calls into question the dichotomy itself. Either/or claims based on isolated Bible verses that have been translated into another language and then used as the source of authority of God's will for your life are very flimsy foundations for your relationship to money.

Whether Jesus was rich or poor is not really the point. The point is: How does this kind of dichotomous thinking affect your relationship to money?

My purpose in this book is to encourage you to go beyond the dichotomies, beyond the Bible verses taken out of context, beyond the certainty that a few words in the Bible on any topic are enough to establish the ultimate truth on anything.

The challenge is to be heroic about money. Heroism responds to a threat. We live in an era in which the primary threat to the economic wellbeing of the majority of people is the growing wealth inequity between the one-percent and the ninety-nine percent.

A hero perceives the threat and sets out to end it, not just for the hero's own benefit, but for the benefit of others. If you have money, you can choose to be heroic about how you use it for the wellbeing of others. If you don't have money, you can choose to be heroic in your effort to face the challenge. In either case, the New Testament gospels are whole stories about a hero who confronted economic inequity at its source of power. They are not constraining rulebooks but liberating stories. Read this way, they can teach you to become a money hero.

Appendix

The Sermon on the Mount
Matthew 5-7

Seeing the crowds, he went up on the mountain, and when he sat down his disciples came to him. And he opened his mouth and taught them, saying:

"Blessed are the poor in spirit, for theirs is the kingdom of heaven.

"Blessed are those who mourn, for they shall be comforted. "Blessed are the meek, for they shall inherit the earth.

"Blessed are those who hunger and thirst for righteousness, for they shall be satisfied.

"Blessed are the merciful, for they shall obtain mercy.

"Blessed are the pure in heart, for they shall see God.

"Blessed are the peacemakers, for they shall be called sons of God.

"Blessed are those who are persecuted for righteousness' sake, for theirs is the kingdom of heaven.

"Blessed are you when men revile you and persecute you and utter all kinds of evil against you falsely on my account.

Rejoice and be glad, for your reward is great in heaven, for so men persecuted the prophets who were before you. "You are the salt of the earth; but if salt has lost its taste, how shall its saltness be restored? It is no longer good for anything except to be thrown out and trodden under foot by men.

"You are the light of the world. A city set on a hill cannot be hid. Nor do men light a lamp and put it under a bushel, but on a stand, and it gives light to all in the house. Let your light so shine before men, that they may see your good works and give glory to your Father who is in heaven.

"Think not that I have come to abolish the law and the prophets; I have come not to abolish them but to fulfill them.

191

For truly, I say to you, till heaven and earth pass away, not an iota, not a dot, will pass from the law until all is accomplished. Whoever then relaxes one of the least of these commandments and teaches men so, shall be called least in the kingdom of heaven; but he who does them and teaches them shall be called great in the kingdom of heaven.

For I tell you, unless your righteousness exceeds that of the scribes and Pharisees, you will never enter the kingdom of heaven.

"You have heard that it was said to the men of old, —You shall not kill; and whoever kills shall be liable to judgment.' But I say to you that every one who is angry with his brother shall be liable to judgment; whoever insults his brother shall be liable to the council, and whoever says, —You fool!' shall be liable to the hell of fire. So if you are offering your gift at the altar, and there remember that your brother has something against you, leave your gift there before the altar and go; first be reconciled to your brother, and then come and offer your gift. Make friends quickly with your accuser, while you are going with him to court, lest your accuser hand you over to the judge, and the judge to the guard, and you be put in prison; truly, I say to you, you will never get out till you have paid the last penny.

"You have heard that it was said, —You shall not commit adultery.' But I say to you that every one who looks at a woman lustfully has already committed adultery with her in his heart. If your right eye causes you to sin, pluck it out and throw it away; it is better that you lose one of your members than that your whole body be thrown into hell. And if your right hand causes you to sin, cut it off and throw it away; it is better that you lose one of your members than that your whole body go into hell.

"It was also said, —Whoever divorces his wife, let him give her a certificate of divorce.' But I say to you that every one who divorces his wife, except on the ground of unchastity, makes her an adulteress; and whoever marries a divorced woman commits adultery.

"Again you have heard that it was said to the men of old, —You shall not swear falsely, but shall perform to the Lord what you have sworn.' But I say to you, Do not swear at all, either by heaven, for it is the throne of God, or by the earth, for it is his footstool, or by Jerusalem, for it is the city of the great King. And do not swear by your head, for you cannot make one hair white or black. Let what you say be simply —Yes' or —No'; anything more than this comes from evil.

"You have heard that it was said, —An eye for an eye and a tooth for a tooth.' But I say to you, Do not resist one who is evil. But if any one strikes you on the right cheek, turn to him the other also; and if any one would sue you and take your coat, let him have your cloak as well; and if any one forces you to go one mile, go with him two miles. Give to him who begs from you, and do not refuse him who would borrow from you.

"You have heard that it was said, —You shall love your neighbor and hate your enemy.' But I say to you, Love your enemies and pray for those who persecute you, so that you may be sons of your Father who is in heaven; for he makes his sun rise on the evil and on the good, and sends rain on the just and on the unjust. For if you love those who love you, what reward have you? Do not even the tax collectors do the same? And if you salute only your brethren, what more are you doing than others? Do not even the Gentiles do the same? You, therefore, must be perfect, as your heavenly Father is perfect.

"Beware of practicing your piety before men in order to be seen by them; for then you will have no reward from your Father who is in heaven. "Thus, when you give alms, sound no trumpet before you, as the hypocrites do in the synagogues and in the streets, that they may be praised by men. Truly, I say to you, they have received their reward. But when you give alms, do not let your left hand know what your right hand is doing, so that your alms may be in secret; and your Father who sees in secret will reward you. "And when you pray, you must not be like the hypocrites; for they love to stand and pray in the synagogues and at the street corners, that they may be seen by men. Truly, I say to you, they have received their reward. But when you pray, go into your room and shut the door and pray to your Father who is in secret; and your Father who sees in secret will reward you. "And in praying do not heap up empty phrases as the Gentiles do; for they think that they will be heard for their many words. Do not be like them, for your Father knows what you need before you ask him.

Pray then like this: Our Father who art in heaven, Hallowed be thy name. Thy kingdom come. Thy will be done, on earth as it is in heaven. Give us this day our daily bread; And forgive us our debts, as we also have forgiven our debtors; And lead us not into temptation, But deliver us from evil. For if you forgive men their trespasses, your heavenly Father also will forgive you; but if you do not forgive men their trespasses, neither will your Father forgive your trespasses.

"And when you fast, do not look dismal, like the hypocrites, for they disfigure their faces that their fasting may be seen by men. Truly, I say to you, they have received their reward. But when you fast, anoint your head and wash your face, that your fasting may not be seen by men but by your Father who is in secret; and your Father who sees in secret will reward you.

"Do not lay up for yourselves treasures on earth, where moth and rust consume and where thieves break in and steal, but lay up for yourselves treasures in heaven, where neither moth nor rust consumes and where thieves do not break in and steal. For where your treasure is, there will your heart be also.

"The eye is the lamp of the body. So, if your eye is sound, your whole body will be full of light; but if your eye is not sound, your whole body will be full of darkness. If then the light in you is darkness, how great is the darkness!

"No one can serve two masters; for either he will hate the one and love the other, or he will be devoted to the one and despise the other. You cannot serve God and mammon.

"Therefore I tell you, do not be anxious about your life, what you shall eat or what you shall drink, nor about your body, what you shall put on. Is not life more than food, and the body more than clothing? Look at the birds of the air: they neither sow nor reap nor gather into barns, and yet your heavenly Father feeds them. Are you not of more value than they? And which of you by being anxious can add one cubit to his span of life. And why are you anxious about clothing? Consider the lilies of the field, how they grow; they neither toil nor spin; yet I tell you, even Solomon in all his glory was not arrayed like one of these. But if God so clothes the grass of the field, which today is alive and tomorrow is thrown into the oven, will he not much more clothe you, O men of little faith? Therefore do not be anxious, saying, —What shall we eat?' or —What shall we drink?' or —What shall we wear?' For the Gentiles seek all these things; and your heavenly Father knows that you need them all. But seek first his kingdom and his righteousness, and all these things shall be yours as well. "Therefore do not be anxious about tomorrow, for tomorrow will be anxious for itself. Let the day's own trouble be sufficient for the day.

"Judge not, that you be not judged. For with the judgment you pronounce you will be judged, and the measure you give will be the measure you get. Why do you see the speck that is in your brother's eye, but do not notice the log that is in your own eye? Or how can you say to your brother, —Let me take the speck out of your eye,' when there is the log in your own eye? You hypocrite, first take the log out of your own eye, and then you will see clearly to take the speck out of your brother's eye.

"Do not give dogs what is holy; and do not throw your pearls before swine, lest they trample them under foot and turn to attack you. "Ask, and it will be given you; seek, and you will find; knock, and it will be opened to you. For every one who asks receives, and he who seeks finds, and to him who knocks it will be opened. Or what man of you, if his son asks him for bread, will give him a stone? Or if he asks for a fish, will give him a serpent? If you then, who are evil, know how to give good gifts to your children, how much more will your Father who is in heaven give good things to those who ask him! So whatever you wish that men would do to you, do so to them; for this is the law and the prophets.

"Enter by the narrow gate; for the gate is wide and the way is easy, that leads to destruction, and those who enter by it are many. For the gate is narrow and the way is hard, that leads to life, and those who find it are few. "Beware of false prophets, who come to you in sheep's clothing but inwardly are ravenous wolves. You will know them by their fruits. Are grapes gathered from thorns, or figs from thistles? So, every sound tree bears good fruit, but the bad tree bears evil fruit. A sound tree cannot bear evil fruit, nor can a bad tree bear good fruit. Every tree that does not bear good fruit is cut down and thrown into the fire. Thus you will know them by their fruits. "Not every one who says to me, —Lord, Lord,' shall enter the kingdom of heaven, but he who does the will of my Father who is in heaven. On that day many will say to me, —Lord, Lord, did we not prophesy in your name, and cast out demons in your name, and do many mighty works in your name?' And then will I declare to them, —I never knew you; depart from me, you evildoers.'

"Every one then who hears these words of mine and does them will be like a wise man who built his house upon the rock; and the rain fell, and the floods came, and the winds blew and beat upon that house, but it did not fall, because it had been founded on the rock. And every one who hears these words of mine and does not do them will be like a foolish man who built his house upon the sand; and the rain fell, and the floods came, and the winds blew and beat against that house, and it fell; and great was the fall of it."

And when Jesus finished these sayings, the crowds were astonished at his teaching, for he taught them as one who had authority, and not as their scribes (Matthew 5-7, Revised Standard Version).

The Sermon on the Plain
Luke 6:17-49

And he came down with them and stood on a level place, with a great crowd of his disciples and a great multitude of people from all Judea and Jerusalem and the seacoast of Tyre and Sidon, who came to hear him and to be healed of their diseases; and those who were troubled with unclean spirits were cured. And all the crowd sought to touch him, for power came forth from him and healed them all.

And he lifted up his eyes on his disciples, and said:

"Blessed are you poor, for yours is the kingdom of God.

"Blessed are you that hunger now, for you shall be satisfied.

"Blessed are you that weep now, for you shall laugh.

"Blessed are you when men hate you, and when they exclude you and revile you, and cast out your name as evil, on account of the Son of man!

Rejoice in that day, and leap for joy, for behold, your reward is great in heaven; for so their fathers did to the prophets.

"But woe to you that are rich, for you have received your consolation.

"Woe to you that are full now, for you shall hunger.

"Woe to you that laugh now, for you shall mourn and weep.

"Woe to you, when all men speak well of you, for so their fathers did to the false prophets.

"But I say to you that hear, Love your enemies, do good to those who hate you, bless those who curse you, pray for those who abuse you. To him who strikes you on the cheek, offer the other also; and from him who takes away your coat do not withhold even your shirt. Give to every one who begs from you; and of him who takes away your goods do not ask them again.

And as you wish that men would do to you, do so to them. "If you love those who love you, what credit is that to you? For even sinners love those who love them. And if you do good to those who do good to you, what credit is that to you? For even sinners do the same. And if you lend to those from whom you hope to receive, what credit is that to you? Even sinners lend to sinners, to receive as much again. But love your enemies, and do good, and lend, expecting nothing in return; and your reward will be great, and you will be sons of the Most High; for he is kind to the ungrateful and the selfish.

Be merciful, even as your Father is merciful. "Judge not, and you will not be judged; condemn not, and you will not be condemned; forgive, and you will be forgiven; give, and it will be given to you; good measure, pressed down, shaken together, running over, will be put into your lap. For the measure you give will be the measure you get back."

He also told them a parable: "Can a blind man lead a blind man? Will they not both fall into a pit? A disciple is not above his teacher, but every one when he is fully taught will be like his teacher. Why do you see the speck that is in your brother's eye, but do not notice the log that is in your own eye? Or how can you say to your brother, —Brother, let me take out the speck that is in your eye,' when you yourself do not see the log that is in your own eye? You hypocrite, first take the log out of your own eye, and then you will see clearly to take out the speck that is in your brother's eye.

"For no good tree bears bad fruit, nor again does a bad tree bear good fruit; for each tree is known by its own fruit. For figs are not gathered from thorns, nor are grapes picked from a bramble bush. The good man out of the good treasure of his heart produces good, and the evil man out of his evil treasure produces evil; for out of the abundance of the heart his mouth speaks.

"Why do you call me —Lord, Lord,' and not do what I tell you? Every one who comes to me and hears my words and does them, I will show you what he is like: he is like a man building a house, who dug deep, and laid the foundation upon rock; and when a flood arose, the stream broke against that house, and could not shake it, because it had been well built. But he who hears and does not do them is like a man who built a house on the ground without a foundation; against which the stream broke, and immediately it fell, and the ruin of that house was great" (Luke 6:17-49, Revised Standard Version).

References

Bennett, Hal Zina. *Write from the Heart: Unleashing the Power of Your Creativity.* Novato, CA: Nataraj Publishing, 1995.

Bonnet, James. *Stealing Fire from the Gods: The Complete Guide to Story for Writers and Filmmakers.* 2nd ed. Studio City, CA: Michael Wiese Productions, 2006.

Campbell, Joseph. *The Hero With A Thousand Faces.* Bollingen Series XVII. 2nd ed. Princeton, NJ: Princeton University Press, 1968.

Cohn, Emily. "Thomas Piketty Is No. 1 on Amazon Right Now." Huffington Post. http://www.huffingtonpost.com/2014/04/22/thomas-piketty-amazon_n_5191566.html (accessed April 22, 2014).

Lenski, Gerhard E. *Power and Privilege: A Theory of Social Stratification.* Chapel Hill: University of North Carolina Press, 1984.

Leonhardt, David, and Quealy, Kevin. "The American Middle Class Is No Longer the World's Richest." Huffington Post. http://www.nytimes.com/2014/04/23/upshot/the-american-middle-class-is-no-longer-the-worlds-richest.html?_r=0 (accessed April 22, 2014).

Moyers, Bill. "Government = Protection Racket for the 1 Percent." Huffington Post. http://www.huffingtonpost.com/2014/04/24/thomas-piketty-income-inequality_n_5207358.html (accessed April 22, 2014).

Online Etymology, liberal.
   http://www.etymonline.com/index.php?allowed_in_frame=
   0&search=liberal&searchmode=none (accessed April 23,
   2014).

Online Etymology, rely.
   http://www.etymonline.com/index.php?allowed_in_frame=
   0&search=rely&searchmode=none (accessed April 23,
   2014).

Online Etymology, strain.
   http://www.etymonline.com/index.php?allowed_in_frame=
   0&search=strain&searchmode=none (accessed April 23,
   2014).

Peck, M. Scott, M.D. *Further Along The Road Less
   Traveled: The Unending Journey Toward Spiritual
   Growth*. New York: Simon & Schuster, 1993.

Reich, Robert. "Raising Taxes on Corporations That Pay
   Their CEOs Royally and Treat Their Workers like
   Serfs." Huffington Post.
   http://www.huffingtonpost.com/robert-reich/raising-
   taxes-on-corporat_b_5190591.html (accessed April
   22, 2014).

Shwetashva. "About Mahatma Gandhi - Simply Stating the
   Facts, Not Even Criticizing Him." Sulekha.com.
   http://creative.sulekha.com/about-mahatma-gandhi-
   simply-stating-the-facts-not-even-criticizing-
   him_190689_blog (accessed April 23, 2014).

Stevenson, Kalinda Rose. *The Vision of Transformation:
   The Territorial Rhetoric of Ezekiel 40-48*. SBL
   Dissertation Series 154. Scholars Press: Atlantic,
   Georgia, 1996.

Vogler, Christopher. *The Writer's Journey: Mythic Structure
   For Writers*. 2nd ed. Studio City, CA: Michael Wiese
   Productions, 1998.

Voytilla, Stuart. *Myth and the Movies: Discovering the
   Mythic Structure of 50 Unforgettable Films*. Studio
   City, CA: Michael Wiese Productions, 1999.

Waetjen, Herman. *A Reordering of Power: A Socio-Political Reading of Mark's Gospel*. Minneapolis: Fortress Press, 1989.

About the Author

Dr. Kalinda Rose Stevenson is an award-winning author, biblical scholar, and former teacher in theological seminaries. She offers a liberating perspective on the connection between mistranslated Bible verses and false identity. Her unique perspective provides solutions to overcome self-conflict, confusion, and shame caused by misuse of the mistranslated Bible verses.

She earned her Ph.D. in Biblical Studies at the Graduate Theological Union in Berkeley, California, in cooperation with the University of California at Berkeley.

She currently lives with her husband in the Las Vegas area of Nevada.

Find out more by visiting her websites
KalindaRoseStevenson.com
DoestheBibleReallySayThat.com

Index

C

H

N

O

S

Y

Z